Certified General
Accountants Association
of Canada

D0555692

# Personal
# Tax Planning
# 2008/2009

Your source for current tax laws,
regulations and trends for
your tax planning needs

**Self-Counsel Press**
*(a division of)*
International Self-Counsel Press Ltd.
Canada      USA

Self-Counsel Press acknowledges the financial support of the Government of Canada through the Book Publishing Industry Development Program (BPIDP) for our publishing activities.

2008/2009 Edition

Printed in Canada.

**Library and Archives Canada Cataloguing in Publication**

Personal tax planning, 2008-2009 / Certified General Accountants Association of Canada. — 3rd ed.

Includes index.
ISBN 978-1-55180-842-0

1. Tax planning—Canada—Popular works. 2. Income tax—Canada—Popular works. I. Certified General Accountants' Association of Canada
KE5682.P47 2008a          343.7105'2          C2008-906681-2
KF6297.ZA2P47 2008a

*Acknowledgements*

The CGA Association offers thanks to Jeff Buckstein, CGA, for revising *Personal Tax Planning*. Thanks also to contributors Howard Gangbar, CGA, Larry Hemeryck, CGA, AMCT, CFP, CPC, Mark Markandu, CGA, Cheryl Mont, CGA, and reviewers Kim Boswell, CGA, Philip Bright, CGA, Chris Deresh, CGA, Rajendra Kushwah, M.Com., CGA, Denise Wright-Ianni, CGA, and Wendy Zhan, CGA.

Many thanks to CGA Ontario, as well as to CCH Canadian Limited, for providing valuable information that was used in this book.

**Self-Counsel Press**
*(a division of)*
International Self-Counsel Press Ltd.

1481 Charlotte Road          1704 North State Street
North Vancouver, BC  V7J 1H1          Bellingham, WA  98225
Canada          USA

# CONTENTS

# INTRODUCTION

The objective of personal tax planning is to minimize or defer income taxes payable, as part of a long-recognized right for taxpayers to organize their financial/taxation affairs in the most beneficial way possible within legal confines. This requires a thorough understanding of Canada's *Income Tax Act*, plus bulletins, circulars and rulings put forth by the Canada Revenue Agency (CRA), along with other events, such as tax rulings in the courts.

This booklet reflects federal legislation to approximately September 15, 2008, plus other draft legislation introduced but not yet passed into law, which are therefore subject to change before final passage.

## General Inclusions/Exclusions

The *Income Tax Act* is a wide-ranging document, dealing with broad issues like income from employment, a business or property, while at the same time outlining specific rules in many areas. There are, for instance, rules dealing with the inclusion in taxable income of items such as:

- employment insurance (EI) benefits received;

5

- annuity payments; and
- receipts from deferred income plans.

Some payments, such as workers' compensation (WC), federal supplements and social assistance payments, are not included in taxable income, but are contained in the calculation of threshold income when determining entitlement to the:

- child tax benefit;
- age credit;
- goods and services tax credit (GST);
- old age security (OAS); and
- some provincial tax credits.

Other amounts are specifically excluded from income for tax purposes. Examples, which are not discussed in this booklet, include, but are not limited to, the following:

- income earned by a member of a First Nations group on a specified reserve;
- civilian and veterans' war pensions or allowances, from Canada or any ally of Her Majesty;
- income earned by Canadian Forces personnel or police officers while serving in certain high-risk overseas destinations, beginning in 2004;
- certain other benefits and awards to members of the Canadian Forces;
- certain personal damage amounts awarded by the courts;
- payments received by qualified individuals, their spouses or common-law partners and dependants under the multi-provincial assistance package for individuals infected with HIV through the blood supply program;
- payments received by a special trust for distribution to Canadians who were infected with the hepatitis C virus through the blood distribution system over a specified period;
- government-related compensation for disaster relief;
- an RCMP pension or compensation received in respect of an injury, disability or death; and
- lottery winnings and other windfalls as defined by the CRA.

Amounts that are exempt from income tax by virtue of a stipulation in a tax convention or agreement with another country with the force of law in Canada are also excluded from income.

## Key Terminology

One term that is often used in this booklet is "arm's length." This term refers to two parties that are free to act independently, with neither considered to have undue influence or control over the other's decisions. Any deal they make is assumed to be fair for income tax purposes. Conversely, certain related parties, which could include persons and/or corporations controlled by them, are not considered to be dealing at arm's length. "Non-arm's-length" transactions are subject to special rules. A special provision of the *Income Tax Act*, for example, automatically reduces an excessive price to fair market value (FMV) in a transaction involving parties that are not dealing at arm's length from each other. Furthermore, such adjustments might lead to a double taxation situation; thus, great care must be taken when not dealing at arm's length.

Another term often used is "rollover," such as a "spousal rollover," where property is transferred from one spouse to another upon death on a tax deferred basis. Various types of rollovers are available under the *Income Tax Act*, and such transactions are often complex, requiring professional assistance.

Readers should also note that social changes over the past few years have contributed toward a broader definition of what constitutes a "spouse." Most references in the *Income Tax Act* now refer to a "spouse or common-law partner." The term spouse means a party to a legal marriage to an opposite-sex partner or, as per legislation passed by the federal government in mid-2005, a same-sex partner. Common-law partner means a person of either the opposite or the same sex who has been cohabiting with the taxpayer in a conjugal relationship for at least one year, or is the natural or adoptive parent of the taxpayer's child.

Personal tax planning includes a concerted effort to minimize or defer taxes payable, a practice that is generally accepted. However, the *Income Tax Act* includes a general anti-avoidance rule (GAAR), which allows the CRA and tax courts to reassess any transaction that is considered to have defeated the object, spirit and purpose of the Act. Under GAAR, for instance, if it appears that a transaction or series of transactions has taken place primarily for the purpose of obtaining a tax benefit, it could be subject to adjustment, particularly if it can be established that its application results in a misuse or abuse of the provisions contained within the Act.

As income tax rules are often complex and ever developing, however, tax planning should be an ongoing process. Taxpayers should, for instance, revise their tax and financial plans as changes occur in government legislation and as personal circumstances dictate. Readers are advised to review specific tax plans with their Certified General Accountant.

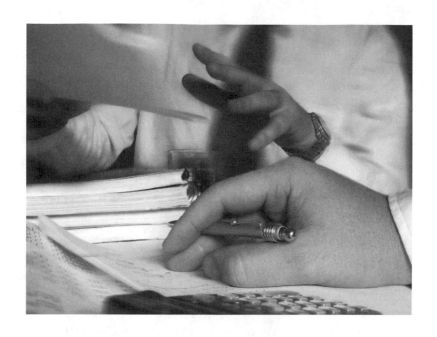

# SUMMARY OF MAJOR 2008 FEDERAL AND PROVINCIAL/TERRITORIAL CHANGES AFFECTING INDIVIDUALS

## Federal

### CPI Adjustment to Income Tax Brackets and Non-Refundable Tax Credits

The taxable income thresholds in all four federal tax brackets were increased by 1.9 per cent in 2008 to mirror changes in the Consumer Price Index (CPI). Furthermore, all indexed non-refundable tax credits also increased by 1.9 per cent in 2008 in order to reflect the CPI adjustment. Please see the chapter on federal and provincial/territorial non-refundable tax credits as well as Appendices I and III for further details.

### Tax-Free Savings Account (TFSA)

The 2008 federal budget introduced a new Tax-Free Savings Account (TFSA) which, beginning in 2009, will allow Canadians who are 18 and older to save up to $5,000 per year in the TFSA investment vehicle. Unlike a registered retirement savings plan (RRSP), investors will not be able to deduct contributions to a TFSA for tax purposes; however, investment income, including capital gains earned within the TFSA will not be subject to tax, even when the funds are ultimately withdrawn.

### Increase in RRSP Annual Contribution Limit

The annual registered retirement savings plan (RRSP) contribution ceiling was raised to $20,000 in 2008, from $19,000 in 2007. It is scheduled to rise to at least $21,000 in 2009 and $22,000 in 2010, after which the annual maximum contribution rates will be indexed to reflect increases in average wage growth.

### Increase in RPP Annual Contribution Limit

Money purchase registered pension plan (RPP) contribution limits increased in 2008 to $21,000, from $20,000 in 2007; they will increase again to at least $22,000 in 2009, after which they will be indexed annually to account for the average wage growth.

The maximum annual contribution limit for defined-benefit RPPs also increased in 2008 to $2,333 per year of service, up from $2,222 in 2007; they will increase again to at least $2,444 in 2009, after which they will be indexed on an annual basis to reflect increases in average wage growth.

### Pension/Work Option

The 2007 federal budget introduced legislation whereby beginning in 2008, certain defined-benefit pension-plan holders who are at least 55 years of age may receive up to 60 per cent of their pension, while still being permitted to accrue further benefits.

### Increase in RESP Time Limits

The 2008 federal budget increased by 10 years the time available for contributors, such as a parent or grandparent, to contribute to a registered education savings plan (RESP) for their child or grandchild. Contributors may now deposit into an RESP plan for a maximum of 31 years — 35 years for a taxpayer that is disabled, up from 21 and 25 years respectively.

The contribution age limit for beneficiaries of family plan RESPs has also increased. No contributions may be made on behalf of a beneficiary who is 31 years of age or older, up from 21 years of age previously.

The deadline for plan termination has also been extended. RESP plans may now stay open for 35 years, 10 years beyond the previous 25-year limit. The new deadline is 40 years for taxpayers who qualify for the disability tax credit (DTC), up from 30 years previously.

## Registered Disability Savings Plan (RDSP)

The 2007 federal budget introduced a new registered disability savings plan (RDSP), which is designed to provide savings for the long-term financial security of a child or adult with a disability who is eligible for the disability tax credit (DTC). This plan is expected to be available by the end of 2008.

As with an RESP, earnings generated on contributions are tax exempt while they remain in the plan. Contributions are not tax deductible, nor are they included in income when paid out. All other amounts paid out of the plan are included in the beneficiary's income. Anyone can contribute to an RDSP with the permission of the holder, and contributions are permitted until the end of the year in which the beneficiary reaches 59. Contributions are limited to a lifetime maximum of $200,000 with no annual limit. Payments from an RDSP must commence by the end of the year in which the beneficiary turns 60.

To augment funds in the RDSP the government will contribute, in the form of Canada Disability Savings Grants (CDSG), funds equivalent to between 100 per cent to 300 per cent of RDSP contributions, to a maximum of $3,500 annually, and $70,000 over the lifetime of the beneficiary, depending on the net income of the beneficiary's family. The federal government will also contribute up to $1,000 annually in Canada Disability Savings Bonds (CDSB), to a maximum of $20,000, depending on the beneficiary's family net income. Beneficiaries must be 49 years of age or younger at the end of the year to be eligible for a CDSG or CDSB.

## Canada Child Tax Benefit Payments (CCTB)

Beginning July 2008, CCTB National Child Benefit supplement (NCB) payments to Canadians rose to $2,025 for the first child (from $1,988), $1,792 for the second child (from $1,758) and $1,704 for each subsequent child (from $1,673).

As a result, the maximum annual benefit under the combined CCTB and NCB supplement increased to $3,332 (from $3,271) for the first child; to $3,099 (from $3,041) for the second child; and $3,102 (from $3,046) for each subsequent child. The maximum indexed Child Disability Benefit (CDB) supplement for parents in low and modest-income families with children who have disabilities and a net family income of less than $37,885 (from $37,178), increased to $2,395 (from $2,351) in 2008.

## Decrease in Goods and Services Tax (GST) Rate

The goods and services tax (GST) rate was reduced by one percentage point, from 6 per cent, down to 5 per cent, effective January 1, 2008.

## Provincial/Territorial

### Major Personal Income Tax Developments in Provincial/Territorial Budgets

Listed below are some of the major items of note that were announced or proposed as a result of the 2008 provincial and territorial budgets. Check with your local Certified General Accountant for an outline of more specific budgetary measures affecting your jurisdiction.

# Alberta:

### Adjustment to Non-Refundable Tax Credits

The taxable income thresholds for all indexed non-refundable tax credits increased by 4.7 per cent in 2008. Please see the chapter on federal and provincial/territorial non-refundable tax credits as well as Appendix I for further details.

### Increase to Disability, Caregiver Tax Credits

The 2008 provincial budget significantly increased — by $5,000 — the disability, disability supplement, infirm dependant and caregiver tax credits. The disability supplement, infirm dependant and caregiver tax credits increased to $9,355, more than doubling the previously scheduled index-adjusted amount of $4,355. The disability credit increased to $12,466 from an index-adjusted $7,466. The upper income threshold amount for the disability supplement, infirm dependant and caregiver tax credits, also increased by $5,000.

These adjustments are retroactive to January 1, 2008.

Please see the chapter on federal and provincial/territorial non-refundable tax credits as well as Appendix I for further details.

### Alberta Family Employment Tax Credit Increased

It was announced in the 2008 provincial budget that the Alberta Family Employment Tax Credit, which provides a refundable credit for certain low-income working families with children under 18, would be increased by 10 per cent, effective July 1, 2008.

The maximum benefit was increased to $669 for families with one child; $1,277 for two children; $1,642 for families with three children; and $1,764 for those with four or more children.

The income level at which this credit begins to phase out also increased — by $5,000 to $32,633.

## Dividend Tax Credits and Small Business Threshold

The dividend tax credit on eligible corporations (i.e., publicly listed Canadian corporations, plus private residential firms that pay Canadian tax at the general corporate rate) was raised from 8 per cent to 9 per cent in 2008. It is scheduled to increase again to 10 per cent in 2009.

The small business dividend tax credit rate dropped to 4.5 per cent in 2008 (from 5.5 per cent in 2007). It is scheduled to decline further, to 3.5 per cent in 2009.

Also, the small business threshold, at which Canadian-Controlled Private Corporation (CCPC) firms are allowed to earn active business income at preferential rates, was increased from $430,000 to $460,000, effective April 1, 2008. A further increase in this CCPC threshold to $500,000 is scheduled for 2009.

## Elimination of Alberta Health Care Premiums Announced for 2009

It was announced in the 2008 provincial budget that Alberta Health Care Insurance Plan premiums would be eliminated as of January 1, 2009.

## Scientific Research and Experimental Development Credit for 2009

Effective January 1, 2009, a new, 10 per cent provincial Scientific Research and Experimental Development Credit will be available on eligible expenditures of up to $4 million.

## Parallel Measures to Federal Initiatives

The Alberta provincial government has paralleled certain measures announced by the federal government, including changes to capital cost allowance (CCA) rates.

# British Columbia:

## Adjustment to Income Tax Brackets and Non-Refundable Tax Credits

The taxable income thresholds for all five provincial tax brackets were increased by 1.8 per cent in 2008. All indexed non-refundable tax credits also increased by 1.8 per cent. Please see the chapter on federal and provincial/territorial non-refundable tax credits as well as Appendices I, III and V for further details.

## Tax Rate Reduction on Most Provincial Income Brackets

British Columbia reduced the tax rates on all but its top taxable provincial income bracket, effective January 1, 2008, as follows:

Between:

| | |
|---|---|
| $0 - $35,016 | Decrease from 5.70 per cent to 5.35 per cent |
| $35,016 - $70,033 | Decrease from 8.65 per cent to 8.15 per cent |
| $70,033 - $80,406 | Decrease from 11.10 per cent to 10.50 per cent |
| $80,406 - $97,636 | Decrease from 13.00 per cent to 12.29 per cent |
| Over $97,636 | Remains at 14.70 per cent |

The province further reduced the bottom two tax rates in the 2008 provincial budget as follows:

Between:

| | |
|---|---|
| $0 - $35,016 | Decrease from 5.35 per cent to 5.24 per cent |
| $35,016 - $70,033 | Decrease from 8.15 per cent to 7.98 per cent |

Then, in the province's economic update they accelerated additional cuts originally scheduled for implementation in 2009 forward to 2008, as follows:

Between:

| | |
|---|---|
| $0 - $35,016 | Decrease from 5.24 per cent to 5.06 per cent |
| $35,016 - $70,033 | Decrease from 7.98 per cent to 7.70 per cent |

Therefore the following rates will apply to British Columbia taxpayers in 2008:

Between:

| | |
|---|---|
| $0 - $35,016 | 5.06 per cent |
| $35,016 - $70,033 | 7.70 per cent |
| $70,033 - $80,406 | 10.50 per cent |
| $80,406 - $97,636 | 12.29 per cent |
| Over $97,636 | 14.70 per cent |

The new low bracket tax rate of 5.06 per cent will therefore also be the new multiplier used for determining the provincial non-refundable tax credits, and other calculations, such as minimum alternative tax, in 2008.

## Introduction of "Revenue-Neutral" Carbon Tax

The 2008 British Columbia provincial budget introduced a carbon tax — the first such wide-scale tax by any jurisdiction in Canada. It starts at

$10 a tonne in 2008 and is being charged for carbon, or carbon equivalent emissions via various sources of fossil fuel, such as gasoline, coal, propane and natural gas within the home and business environment.

This tax will be increased by $5 a tonne over the next four years, until it reaches $30 by July 1, 2012.

Over a period of time, the carbon tax is designed to be "revenue neutral" in that the revenue the government expects to raise from this measure will be returned to individuals and businesses via tax cuts.

This tax took effect July 1, 2008. Prior to that date, the government provided most residents of B.C. with a one-time "Climate Action Dividend" of $100. A supplementary credit of $100 per adult and $30 per child, or $100 for the first child in a single parent family, was also made available to certain lower income individuals and families, together with their federal goods and services (GST) credit. This supplementary credit will also be available in future years.

### Parallel Measures to Federal Initiatives

The British Columbia provincial government has paralleled certain measures announced by the federal government, including introducing an amendment to the British Columbia *Pension Benefits Standards Act* that will allow certain holders of registered pension plans as early as 55 years of age the opportunity to begin receiving up to 60 per cent of their pension, while still being permitted to accrue further benefits.

## Manitoba:

### Tax Reduction on Middle Tax Band

The rate in Manitoba's middle income tax bracket has declined from 13 per cent to 12.75 per cent, effective January 1, 2008. This affects taxable incomes between $30,544 and $66,000. The top bracket threshold also increased, by $1,000, to $66,000 in 2008.

In 2009, the rate in the lowest tax bracket is scheduled to reduce from 10.9 per cent to 10.8 per cent. The middle tax bracket threshold amount is scheduled to increase from $30,544 to $31,000, and the top tax bracket threshold is scheduled to increase from $66,000 to $67,000.

### Introduction of a Primary Caregiver Tax Credit in 2009

The 2008 provincial budget introduced a new, refundable Primary Caregiver Tax Credit, which is set to commence in 2009. This credit will provide up to $1,020 annually to certain non-remunerated caregivers who are providing assistance related to a health and/or disability issue, including palliative care, to a relative, neighbour or friend.

### Parallel Measures to Federal Initiatives

Certain provincial tax measures designed to parallel initiatives announced by the federal government will also take effect in Manitoba in 2008, such as a one-year extension of the Manitoba Mineral Exploration Tax Credit to encompass flow-through share agreements entered into up to and including March 31, 2009, and special capital cost allowance rates for manufacturers.

## New Brunswick:

### Adjustment to Income Tax Brackets and Non-Refundable Tax Credits

The taxable income thresholds for all four provincial tax brackets were increased by 1.9 per cent in 2008. All indexed non-refundable tax credits also increased by 1.9 per cent. Please see the chapter on federal and provincial/territorial non-refundable tax credits as well as Appendices I, III and V for further details.

## Newfoundland and Labrador:

### Adjustment to Income Tax Brackets and Non-Refundable Tax Credits

The taxable income thresholds for all three provincial tax brackets, as well as the province's non-refundable tax credits, were increased by an average of 1 per cent in 2007 to reflect one-half of a 2 per cent increase that went into effect on July 1, 2007. In 2008, the full 2 per cent increase took effect.

Please see the chapter on federal and provincial/territorial non-refundable tax credits as well as Appendices I, III and V for further details.

### Tax Rate Reduction on All Provincial Income Brackets

Newfoundland and Labrador reduced its tax rates in all three income brackets in 2007. Effective July 1, 2007, the rates decreased as follows:

Between:

| | |
|---|---|
| $0 - $29,886 | Decrease from 10.57 per cent to 8.70 per cent |
| $29,886 - $59,772 | Decrease from 16.16 per cent to 13.80 per cent |
| Over $59,772 | Decrease from 18.02 per cent to 16.50 per cent |

In its 2008 budget, the province announced further reductions of 1 per cent effective July 1, 2008, on the following indexed tax brackets:

Between:

| | |
|---|---|
| $0 - $30,215 | Decrease from 8.70 per cent to 7.70 per cent |
| $30,215 - $60,429 | Decrease from 13.80 per cent to 12.80 per cent |
| Over $60,429 | Decrease from 16.50 per cent to 15.50 per cent |

Therefore the average rates for 2008 are as follows:

Between:

| | |
|---|---|
| $0 - $30,215 | 8.20 per cent |
| $30,215 - $60,429 | 13.30 per cent |
| Over $60,429 | 16.00 per cent |

The new low bracket tax rate of 8.20 per cent is therefore also the new multiplier used for determining the provincial non-refundable tax credits, and other calculations, such as minimum alternative tax, in 2008.

### Elimination of Provincial Surtax

The 9 per cent surtax on provincial threshold tax of $7,102 was eliminated on July 1, 2007. Therefore no provincial surtax applies in 2008.

### Increase in Benefit Thresholds

Effective July 1, 2008, the income threshold range at which the Newfoundland and Labrador Seniors' Benefit phase out begins and ends has been increased from a range of $15,333 to $21,920, to a new range of $25,275 to $31,930 for individual taxpayers; the maximum credit was also more than doubled from $384 to $776. The same payment and qualifying income threshold also applies to senior couples.

This benefit is a refundable tax credit for lower income seniors, who turn 65 during the calendar year, or are older.

## Northwest Territories:

### Adjustment to Income Tax Brackets and Non-Refundable Tax Credits

The taxable income thresholds for all four territorial tax brackets were increased by 1.9 per cent in 2008. All indexed non-refundable tax credits also increased by 1.9 per cent. Please see the chapter on federal and provincial/territorial non-refundable tax credits as well as Appendices I, III and V for further details.

# Nova Scotia:

## Adjustment to Income Tax Brackets and Non-Refundable Tax Credits

The basic personal amount rose $250 to $7,731 in 2008 as part of a scheduled $1,000 increase over the four years between 2007 and 2010, inclusive. The amounts for certain non-refundable tax credits, including the spousal, age, dependant, pension, disability and caregiver amounts, also increased as part of a scheduled 13.83 per cent rise between 2007 and 2010. Please see the chapter on federal and provincial/territorial non-refundable tax credits as well as Appendices I, III and V for further details.

## Increase in Volunteer Firefighters Tax Credit

The refundable Volunteer Firefighters Tax Credit introduced for the 2007 taxation year was increased from $250 to $375 in 2008. It will further increase to $500 in 2009.

## New Volunteer Ground Search and Rescue Tax Credit

A new, refundable provincial tax credit for volunteer ground search and rescuers was established in 2008 at rates equivalent to those provided volunteer firefighters. This credit is worth $375 in 2008, increasing to $500 in 2009.

## Doubling of Graduate Tax Credit

The provincial government's annual Graduate Tax Credit for graduates of eligible post-secondary programs doubled from $1,000 to $2,000, effective January 1, 2008.

## Expansion of Healthy Living Tax Credit

The provincial government announced that Nova's Scotia's Healthy Living Tax Credit, which is currently $500 and covers certain sporting and recreational activities of children under 18, will be expanded in 2009 to encompass all residents of Nova Scotia.

## Parallel Measures to Federal Initiatives

It was also announced in the provincial budget that the province will match the federal government's transit tax credit, applied against provincial rates, beginning in 2009.

# Nunavut:

## Adjustment to Income Tax Brackets and Non-Refundable Tax Credits

The taxable income thresholds for all four territorial tax brackets were increased by 1.9 per cent in 2008. Furthermore, all indexed non-refundable tax credits also increased by 1.9 per cent. Please see the chapter on federal and provincial/territorial non-refundable tax credits as well as Appendices I, III and V for further details.

## Voluntary Firefighters Tax Credit

The 2008 territorial budget introduced a new $500 tax credit for volunteer firefighters who complete at least 200 hours of community service per year. The Volunteer Firefighters Tax Credit is effective January 1, 2008.

## Parallel Measures to Federal Initiatives

The Nunavut territorial government has paralleled various measures announced by the federal government, including doubling to $2,000 the pension income amount eligible for territorial credit, and introducing textbook credits of $65 and $20 for eligible full-time and part-time post-secondary students, respectively. Both measures are effective January 1, 2008.

# Ontario:

## Increased Threshold for All Income Tax Brackets and Non-Refundable Tax Credits

The taxable income thresholds for all three provincial tax brackets were increased by 1.5 per cent in 2008. Furthermore, all indexed non-refundable tax credits also increased by 1.5 per cent. Please see the chapter on federal and provincial/territorial non-refundable tax credits as well as Appendices I, III and V for further details.

## Increase in Ontario Child Benefit

The 2007 provincial budget introduced an Ontario Child Benefit (OCB), effective July 1, 2007, for each child under 18. The OCB will ultimately replace the Ontario Child Care Supplement for Working Families (OCCS) benefit as well as most child-related social assistance benefits. This process began in 2008.

The initial OCB payment was $250 (in addition to social assistance or OCCS payments), reduced by 3.4 per cent of adjusted family net income over $20,000. That amount was increased to $600 on July 1, 2008, reduced by 8 per cent of adjusted family net income in excess of $20,000.

## Land Transfer Tax Refund Program

The province's December 2007 Fall Economic Outlook and Fiscal Review, or mini-budget, expanded the provisions of Ontario's existing Land Transfer Tax Refund available to first-time purchasers of newly constructed homes to encompass first-time homebuyers of resale homes as well. Effective December 14, 2007, first-time purchasers of both types of homes are now eligible for a provincial refund on up to $2,000 of the land transfer tax paid for their home.

## Increase in Small Business Deduction Threshold

The province's 2007 mini-budget in December 2007 increased Ontario's small business deduction threshold rate from $400,000 to $500,000, retroactive to January 1, 2007.

## Parallel Measures to Federal Initiatives

The Ontario provincial government has paralleled certain measures announced by the federal government, including enhancing the limits of the province's Ontario Innovation Tax Credit (OITC) to follow improvements made to the federal Scientific Research and Experimental Development (SR&ED) tax credit, and various capital cost allowance measures.

# Prince Edward Island:

## Adjustment to Income Tax Brackets and Certain Non-Refundable Tax Credits

The taxable income thresholds for all three provincial tax brackets were increased by an average of 2 per cent in 2007 to reflect one-half of a 4 per cent increase that went into effect on July 1, 2007. In addition, certain of the province's non-refundable tax credits — involving the basic personal amount, spousal and age amounts — also increased by an average of 2 per cent in 2007. In 2008, the full 4 per cent increase took effect.

Please see the chapter on federal and provincial/territorial non-refundable tax credits as well as Appendices I, III and V for further details.

## Provincial Surtax Threshold Raised

The threshold level at which Prince Edward Island's 10 per cent surtax on provincial tax will be levied has been raised from $8,850 of basic provincial tax to $12,500 of provincial tax in 2008.

### Tax Relief Offered to Farmers

The Provincial Treasury announced in July 2008 that tax relief was being offered to farmers in Prince Edward Island via "an immediate 25 per cent depreciation on the assessment of all farm buildings specifically designed and used for the production of pork, beef, and potatoes."

It also said that farmers will be permitted to "apply for assessment reductions for any farm buildings that can no longer be used for their original purpose."

## Quebec:

### Increase in Tax Brackets

The taxable income thresholds in all three provincial tax brackets were increased. The lowest 16 per cent bracket applies to taxable income of $37,500 or less; the 20 per cent middle bracket covers taxable income between $37,500 and $75,000. Income above $75,000 will be taxed at the top provincial marginal rate of 24 per cent.

### Increase in Basic Credit

The 2008 basic provincial credit increased from $9,745 to $10,215. The basic credit is now a single amount and no longer split between amounts designated for recognized essential needs, plus a complementary amount.

### New Refundable Tax Credit for Persons Giving Respite to Informal Caregivers

The 2008 provincial budget introduced a new refundable tax credit to cover respite expenses of informal caregivers worth up to 30 per cent of $5,200, or $1,560, effective January 1, 2008. This amount, which is reduced by 3 per cent of the caregiver's family income in excess of $50,000, will be indexed in future years.

### Enhancement of the Refundable Tax Credit for Home Support of the Elderly

The tax credit for home support of elderly persons has increased from 25 per cent of up to $15,000 per year, or $3,750, to 30 per cent of an increased $15,600, or $4,680. For seniors who are dependant because of a medical condition, this credit has been increased to 30 per cent of $21,600 or $6,480.

This tax credit is reduced by three per cent of every dollar of family income in excess of $50,000.

### Enhancement of the Tax Credits for Assisted Human Reproduction and Adoption

The 2008 provincial budget increased the rate of the refundable tax credit for the treatment of infertility and adoption expenses from 30 per cent to 50 per cent of up to $20,000, for a maximum credit of $10,000.

### New Adapted Work Premium

The new Adapted Work Premium, which was introduced in the 2008 provincial budget, will be paid to Quebec residents who have a severely limited capacity to secure employment, for reasons such as a severe and prolonged impairment in physical or mental functions. The premiums paid are reduced by 10 per cent of net household work income.

The maximum premium amounts for 2008 are (rounded to the nearest dollar):

|  |  | Reduction threshold | Cut-off threshold |
|---|---|---|---|
| Single person living alone | $1,003 | $12,346 | $22,377 |
| Couple without children | 1,477 | 17,606 | 32,371 |
| Single parent family | 2,787 | 12,346 | 40,211 |
| Couple with children | 3,281 | 17,606 | 50,418 |

### Indexing of the Age Tax Credit Beginning in 2009

The age tax credit, which is currently 20 per cent of $2,200, will be indexed annually beginning in 2009.

### Pension Increases Beginning in 2009

The maximum retirement income eligible for Quebec's provincial tax credit will be increased from $1,500 to $1,750 in 2009; then to $2,000 in 2010. Beginning in 2011, that amount will then be automatically indexed in future years.

### Enhancement of the Refundable Tax Credit for Child Care Expenses

The 2008 provincial budget increased — effective in 2009 — the rate of the refundable tax credit for child care expenses to 60 per cent of expenses for family incomes from $46,755 to $82,100. This credit will then decline to a minimum rate of 26 per cent at an income ceiling of $100,550 (up from $85,535).

# Saskatchewan:

## Adjustment to Income Tax Brackets and Non-Refundable Tax Credits

The taxable income thresholds for all three provincial tax brackets were increased by 1.9 per cent in 2008. Furthermore, all indexed non-refundable tax credits also increased by 1.9 per cent. Please see the chapter on federal and provincial/territorial non-refundable tax credits as well as Appendices I, III and V for further details.

## Adjustment to Basic Personal and Spousal Exemptions, and Child Amount

Saskatchewan's mid-year economic statement increased the basic personal and spousal exemptions by $4,000 — each from $8,945 to $12,945. It also increased the child tax credit by $2,000, from $2,795 to $4,795.

## Increase in Disability-Related Tax Credits

The 2008 provincial budget increased the amount of four disability-related tax credits to $8,190, effective January 1, 2008. These include: the disability credit amount, which increased from an indexed $7,021; as well as the disability supplement for children under 18; the credit for dependants 18 and older due to mental or physical infirmity; and the caregiver amount, all of which increased from an indexed $4,095. Please see the chapter on federal and provincial/territorial non-refundable tax credits as well as Appendix I for further details.

## Increase in Small Business Income Threshold

The income threshold at which preferential tax rates accrue to small businesses which qualify as CCPCs in Saskatchewan increased from $450,000 to $500,000 on July 1, 2008.

## Graduate Retention Program (GRP)

A new provincial Graduate Retention Program (GRP) was introduced, effective January 1, 2008, to replace the Graduate Tax Exemption (GTE) announced in 2007. This new refundable income tax credit rebates up to $20,000 of tuition fees paid by graduates of approved programs from an eligible post-secondary institution in the province. In some cases, it may also apply to Saskatchewan residents who graduate from approved programs at eligible institutions outside the province.

This rebate provides up to: $3,000 for the successful completion of a one-year certificate, diploma or journeyperson program; $6,400 for recipients of a two-year certificate or diploma; $15,000 for students who receive a three-year undergraduate degree; and $20,000 for recipients of a four-year undergraduate degree.

Transition provisions, including a reduced rebate, may apply for some students who graduate with a three- or four-year undergraduate degree in 2008, or a four-year undergraduate degree in 2009. The maximum rebate will be applicable for all students who graduate in 2010 or later.

Benefits will be paid out over a seven-year period, as graduates must remain in Saskatchewan for at least seven years in order to qualify for the full rebate.

### Active Saskatchewan Families Benefit

The 2008 provincial budget announced that a new refundable Active Saskatchewan Families Benefit will provide a rebate of up to $150 a year on behalf of children between the ages of 6 and 14, inclusive, who take part in certain cultural, recreational and sports activities, beginning in 2009.

### Parallel Measure to Federal Initiatives

The Saskatchewan government announced that it would parallel certain measures undertaken by the federal government, such as reintroduction of the Mineral Exploration Tax Credit, to cover transactions that take place after March 31, 2008.

## Yukon:

### Adjustment to Income Tax Brackets and Non-Refundable Tax Credits

The taxable income thresholds for all four territorial tax brackets were increased by 1.9 per cent in 2008. Certain indexed non-refundable tax credits — including the age amount, disability amount, infirm dependant amounts, caregiver, and adoption amounts — also increased by 1.9 per cent. The basic personal amount, and spouse and equivalent-to-spouse amounts all remained at $9,600 — reflecting increases made in response to last year's federal mini-budget.

Please see the chapter on federal and provincial/territorial non-refundable tax credits as well as Appendices I, III and V for further details.

### Parallel Measures to Federal Initiatives

The Yukon territorial government has paralleled various measures announced by the federal government. In the latter part of 2007, for instance, they introduced a $2,000 child tax credit and announced a Yukon Child Fitness Tax Credit of up to $500 per child.

# PART ONE: INCOME AND EXPENSES

## EMPLOYMENT INCOME, EXPENSES AND ALLOWABLE DEDUCTIONS

### Taxable Benefits Derived from Employment Income

The value of most benefits derived from employment is included in personal income. Among the myriad benefits which generally must be included in income are the following:

- tips and gratuities must be reported as income, even though they may not necessarily be included by employers on the employee's T4 slip;

- employees who are awarded near-cash merchandise such as a gift certificate must take the fair market value of that award into account as taxable income;

- subsidized long-term accommodation provided by an employer for the employee's benefit;
- the value of a discount on university tuition fees offered by an employer to spouses and children of employees would normally be considered employment income and therefore represent a taxable benefit to employees (however, if the employer provided a scholarship award directly to the student, that might not be taxable);
- an employee or ex-employee who receives periodic payments under a disability insurance plan, sickness or accident insurance plan or income maintenance insurance plan to compensate for loss of income from an office or employment must include that amount in income if the plan's premiums were paid for by the employer. However, they may deduct from income any amount they may have personally contributed toward such a plan; and
- employees who exercise an option to purchase an automobile from their employer at less than its fair market value (FMV) are considered to have received a taxable benefit for the difference between the price paid and FMV.

## Tax Tips

Flexible employee benefit programs, which allow employees to custom design their own package of health and other benefits, are now very popular in the workplace. Care should be taken when structuring such plans, however, because taxable benefits can result. If, for example, an employee accumulates flex credits and those benefits are received in cash, that amount is generally considered taxable income.

## Non-Taxable Benefits Derived from Employment Income

Although most benefits derived from employment must be included in personal income, there are some exceptions. These include: employers' contributions to private health service plans; group sickness or accident plans; registered pension plans (RPP); and deferred profit sharing plans (DPSP).

Other examples of non-taxable benefits include, but are not limited to:

- ordinary discounts on the employer's merchandise, available to all employees on a non-discriminatory basis;
- subsidized meals available to all employees, provided a reasonable charge is made to cover direct costs;

- the cost for distinctive uniforms, protective clothing or footwear required to be worn during employment, including related laundry expenses;

- reimbursement of moving expenses upon relocation;

- receipt of up to two non-cash gifts (e.g., for Christmas, wedding, birthday) in one year, for certain items and under certain conditions, with a total cost to the employer not exceeding $500, including all applicable taxes;

- receipt of up to two non-cash awards (e.g., for meeting or exceeding targets, reaching a milestone in years of service) in one year, for certain items and under certain conditions, with a total cost to the employer not exceeding $500, including all applicable taxes;

- use of the employer's recreational facilities, or employer-sponsored membership in a social or athletic club, where such membership is considered all or primarily beneficial to the employer (despite the employer not being able to deduct the cost of such fees);

- an employer-mandated medical examination required as a condition of employment;

- employer-sponsored personal counselling services in respect of the mental or physical health of an employee or a person related to an employee, re-employment or retirement;

- employer-sponsored travel where the trip was undertaken predominantly for business reasons;

- employer-sponsored training costs that are work-related;

- tuition and related fees, if the course is required for employment and is primarily for the employer's benefit;

- a reasonable per-kilometre automobile allowance;

- employer-paid cellular phones and other such hand-held devices, as long as they were used primarily for business purposes;

- board, lodging and transportation to special worksites involving duties of a temporary nature, or to remote worksite venues away from the general community where the employee is required to be a reasonable distance away from their principal residence for at least 36 hours;

- a reasonable employer-provided allowance for an employee's child to live at and attend the nearest suitable school, if one is not close to where their parents must reside for employment purposes;

- employer-paid expenses for moving an employee and his or her family, along with their household effects, out of a remote location upon the termination of employment; and
- exclusive on-site child care services provided by employers to all employees for minimal or no cost.

## Tax Tips

If you receive more than two non-cash gifts or awards from your employer, select the two with an aggregate cost closest to $500 as your entitlement. For example, if you received four awards that cost $300, $200, $150 and $100 respectively, select the first two awards (costing $500) as being non-taxable and declare the $250 cost of the remaining two as a taxable benefit.

If you use air miles earned from an incentive program for personal use, you will be deemed to have received a taxable benefit if those points were earned as a result of expenditures paid for by your employer. To avoid that situation, you should be careful to use such air miles strictly for business purposes on behalf of your employer.

Non-taxable expenses for a temporary work site might apply for varying lengths of time, such as a week, a month or a year. The key is that they apply for a reasonable and determinate period of time, generally with about a two-year maximum (although this could vary), with a scheduled date of return to the employee's regular place of employment.

The CRA has ruled that there is no taxable benefit to an employee in a situation where their employer arranges for them to purchase discounted fitness pass memberships from a third party.

If you are an emergency services volunteer, the first $1,000 in payment you receive from a government, municipality or other public authority may be tax free.

## Special Considerations Related to Taxable and Non-taxable Employment Income

Other current issues with respect to the taxability and non-taxability of employee benefits include, but are certainly not limited to, the following points:

- An employer-provided computer and Internet service might not represent a taxable benefit under certain circumstances if employees require such a service to carry out their business obligations. However, the costs associated with purchasing an employer-funded computer that the employee also uses for personal reasons would likely result in a taxable benefit;
- Taxpayers that receive an arbitration award from their employer for reasons such as a collective agreement breach to compensate for lost wages, or receive retroactive payments as a result of a

decision such as pay equity — a component of which might constitute damages — should consult a Certified General Accountant to determine the appropriate tax treatment for that payment;

- In some cases, the courts may be more lenient towards an employee than a shareholder in terms of any benefit amount deemed to be non-taxable. For instance, an employee might be able to exclude 100 per cent of membership fees in a golf club if their membership is primarily for the benefit of their employer. On the other hand, a corporate shareholder might have to apportion the tax-exempt and taxable portion of their fees between business and personal use, respectively. Taxpayers — especially those with a dual employee/shareholder role — should clarify the proper tax treatment with their Certified General Accountant;

- Although child care expenses that have been paid for by an employer are generally considered a taxable benefit, if an employee is required to travel out of town on employment-related business and, as a result, incurs additional child care expenses that are reimbursed by their employer, that amount will not be a taxable benefit;

- If a spouse accompanies an employee on a business trip, and the employer reimburses their travel expenses, that payment is a taxable benefit to the employee unless their spouse was engaged primarily in business activities on behalf of the employer during that trip;

- Any accumulated credit used under a frequent flyer program during a business trip is taxable to the employee and included in their income; and

- Certain members of the clergy or religious organizations are entitled to exclude from income reasonable allowances with respect to transportation expenses in the discharge of their duties.

## Employee Stock Options

Employees who acquire certain publicly listed shares under employee stock option plans are entitled to defer the associated stock option benefit, subject to an annual $100,000 vesting limit, until such shares are disposed of. This deferral is available for shares acquired after February 27, 2000, but is also subject to certain conditions.

If all conditions have been met and the employee elects to defer the tax, they must file a letter by January 15 of the year after the share is acquired (i.e., January 15, 2009, for shares acquired in 2008), complete with the following information:

- a request to have the deferral provisions apply;
- the stock option benefit amount related to the deferred shares;
- confirmation the employee was resident in Canada when the shares were acquired; and
- confirmation that the $100,000 annual vesting limit has not been exceeded.

The tax consequences with respect to stock option plan shares exercised after February 27, 2000, can be quite complicated. For example, special rules might apply that create a deemed dividend and a capital loss.

Holders of employee stock options exercised prior to February 28, 2000, were subject to the long-standing rule that during the year they exercised such an option, the excess of the stock's fair market value (FMV) at the date acquired, over the option's exercise price, was taxable as employment income and must be added to the cost base of shares. Any subsequent gain or loss on disposal — measured from the cost base — was a capital gain or loss.

There were, however, also a series of complex exceptions to that rule, and holders of stock option shares exercised on or after February 28, 2000, that do not qualify for the deduction are still subject to those rules and exceptions.

Consult your Certified General Accountant for details about the correct treatment for stock options or other arrangements, such as exercising warrants to buy or sell shares from an employer.

## Deferred Compensation

A deferred compensation agreement is an agreement to pay wages at a later date for services rendered now. However, the *Income Tax Act* does not allow employees to defer income recognition until it is received. Remuneration that would have been paid had the employee not opted to defer it must be included in the employee's income and also deducted by the employer.

This eliminates the potential income tax advantages that could arise from funded and unfunded deferral plans that are based on unlikely contingencies. When the receipt of funds is subject to contingencies, those conditions will be ignored and the employee taxed unless there is a substantial risk the contingency will not occur, with the amount therefore forfeited.

Deferred signing bonuses may also be considered part of a salary deferral arrangement unless the employment contract stipulates that the employee must render additional services in exchange for earning that extra amount.

Specifically excluded from the definition of salary deferral arrangements are:

- registered pension funds or plans;
- disability or income maintenance insurance plans under policies with insurance companies;
- deferred profit sharing plans (DPSP);
- employee profit sharing plans;
- employee trusts;
- group sickness or accident insurance plans;
- supplementary unemployment benefit plans;
- vacation pay trusts;
- plans or arrangements established for the sole purpose of providing education or training to employees to improve work-related skills;
- plans or arrangements established to defer the salary or wages of a professional athlete;
- employee bonus plans under which employees receive their annual bonuses within three years of the applicable year end; and
- prescribed plans or arrangements, such as sabbatical plans or deferred salary leave plans (DSLP).

Individuals that participate in a deferred salary leave plan must return to their regular employment following a leave of absence for a period that is at least as long as the leave itself. Otherwise any deferred amounts, plus unpaid interest, immediately become taxable as employment income, whether paid out or not, during the taxation year the taxpayer realizes they can't return to work for the specified period.

If employees have the opportunity to obtain additional vacation time via flex credits or payroll deductions, and that vacation time is carried forward until the next calendar year, the CRA has warned this might be considered a salary deferral arrangement for tax purposes.

Salary deferral arrangement taxation rules might also apply when employees take a funded leave of absence just prior to retirement due to unused credits provided under a flex plan. See your Certified General Accountant for details.

## Deductions from Employment Income

Employment income deductions are restricted to those items specifically provided for in the *Income Tax Act*. Besides automobile and legal expenses, which are discussed in the next chapter, other deductible expenses may include:

- employment-related travel expenses, including parking, taxis, bus fare, etc., if required by the terms of employment and not reimbursed;

- office rent and expenses, if the employee and employer have agreed that the employee is to provide their own working environment. It must be their principal workplace or used exclusively, on a regular and continuous basis, for activities such as business-related meetings. If the qualified workspace is in the employee's home, the employee may be allowed a pro-rata deduction for rent paid, maintenance, utilities and minor repairs. Expenses related to mortgage interest, property taxes and insurance may not be deducted (unless, in the case of property taxes and home insurance premiums, they are related to commission sales expenses). To the extent that a claim for workspace in the home exceeds employment income, that portion of the deduction is denied in the current year; however, it may be carried forward indefinitely against future income resulting from the same employment;

- an assistant's salary and supplies, if required to be paid without reimbursement by the terms of employment;

- musical instruments — capital cost allowance (CCA) and related rental, insurance and maintenance costs may be claimed only against income earned directly from using the musical instrument;

- aircraft — CCA, interest expense and operating and maintenance costs related to business use;

- union dues and professional fees if required to maintain membership; and

- expenses of up to two-thirds of earned income for attendant care expenses necessary for a medically impaired person to earn business or employment income. Form T2201 is required when making this claim. (Note: this amount potentially reduces the availability of any medical expense credit for full-time attendant care.)

Apprentice mechanics of self-propelled motor vehicles can write off expenses for tools of the trade acquired after 2001. The amount eligible for write-off is that by which the annual cost of tools (plus the last three months of the previous year, if it represents the first year of employment) exceeds the greater of $1,000, or 5 per cent of the apprentice's related income for that year. Amounts not used can be carried forward for deduction in a subsequent taxation year.

Additional provisions are available for various tradespersons to claim an additional credit of up to $500. Apprentice vehicle mechanics can deduct this amount on top of existing write-off opportunities.

Employers must complete Form T2200 — *Declaration of Conditions of Employment,* to legitimize these deductions.

Employees and partners claiming expenses on their tax returns may be entitled to claim a refund for the business use portion of the GST paid. The GST rebate must then be reported as income in the year it is received. To claim a refund, Form GST 370 must be completed. For a copy of this form and more information, obtain the CRA's *Completion Guide and Form for Employee and Partner GST Rebate.*

Certain members of the clergy or religious organizations may be entitled to deduct an amount paid for living accommodations. They must complete Form T1223 in order to determine that amount. Special rules for expense deductions might also apply to employees such as artists and those who are required to move temporarily to a work camp for their jobs, like individuals involved in forestry operations.

Consult your Certified General Accountant for details.

## Tax Tips

Union dues don't necessarily have to be paid to a Canadian organization. Therefore, employment-related annual dues paid to a trade union outside Canada might also be tax deductible.

A computer used by a professor to teach and create music was ruled to be a musical instrument, and thus eligible for employment deductions, by the tax courts.

An assistant's salary might include that paid to a spouse or other family member if the salary is reasonable for the amount of work performed.

If required by your employer to work at home after business hours, deductions might be available in certain instances if employment after hours is considered by an employer and/or union to constitute a separate working arrangement.

## Commission Sales Expenses

Commissioned salespeople, if required by contract to pay their own expenses, may be able to deduct those expenses against commission income. To do so, both the employee and employer must complete portions of Form T2200.

Commissioned employees are allowed a broader range of deductions than other employees in areas such as advertising, promotion, meals and entertainment. Furthermore, commissioned salespeople, unlike other employees, are allowed to deduct a pro-rata share of property taxes and home insurance premiums against commission income if their workspace is in their home. Such deductions are generally limited to offsetting the amount of commissions earned.

Although the restrictions for commissioned employees are mainly similar to those for salaried employees, there are notable exceptions. For instance, CCA (a full description of Capital Cost Allowance can be found on page 58) on an automobile or aircraft used for business may be deducted against other income to the extent that it has already been utilized to fully reduce commission income, with any residue allowable as a non-capital loss. The interest paid on money borrowed to purchase such an automobile or aircraft may also be deducted.

## Tax Tips

If your expenses exceed commission-related income, there may be alternative methods of making claims available to you. Consult your Certified General Accountant for advice on how to maximize tax savings.

If you are a commissioned employee, consider leasing rather than purchasing capital equipment (such as a computer) where CCA is not allowed.

Commissioned life insurance salespersons are allowed to deduct commissions earned with respect to the purchase of their own policies.

Commissioned sales employees who work in their homes should ensure that a separate business telephone line exists in order for regular phone expenses, other than business long-distance charges, to be deductible.

Additional expense deduction provisions might be available to certain employees who sell property or negotiate contracts on behalf of their employer, provided they normally work away from the employer's office, must pay their own expenses and are remunerated in whole or in part by commissions. Contact your Certified General Accountant for details.

# OTHER TAXABLE BENEFITS

## Use of Company Cars

An employee or shareholder using a company car for strictly business purposes does not incur a taxable benefit.

However, where the automobile involves a degree of personal use, a taxable benefit does occur. A standby charge consisting of 2 per cent of the automobile's original cost (1.5 per cent for a car salesperson), or two-thirds of the lease cost, plus GST, applies for each month the automobile is available for the employee's personal use.

If personal use of the automobile does not exceed 20,000 kilometres annually, and the automobile is used for business more than 50 per cent of the time, a proportional standby charge reduction is permitted. If, for example, a vehicle was driven 40,000 kilometres, including 25,000 kilometres for business (more than half), and 15,000 for personal purposes, the actual standby charge would be calculated as 75 per cent (15,000 divided by 20,000) of the regular standby charge.

When both the employer and employee/shareholder have contributed toward purchasing an automobile, its cost for the purposes of calculating a standby charge would be reduced by the amount paid by the employee/shareholder.

Where an employer is primarily engaged in selling or leasing luxury automobiles, special considerations involving the value of multiple automobiles might have to be taken into account when calculating the standby charge calculation. Please consult your Certified General Accountant for further details if this affects you.

In addition to the standby charge, the employee must calculate an operating benefit, using one of two options.

In 2008, they may elect to make a general declaration of 24 cents per kilometre for personal use (up from 22 cents in 2007); 21 cents per kilometre if selling or leasing automobiles constitutes their principal source of employment (up from 19 cents in 2007). Alternatively, if the car is used more than 50 per cent for business, the deemed operating benefit may be one-half of the standby charge, provided the employee notifies their employer in writing before the end of the year. As with other taxable benefits, GST is deemed to be included in the operating benefit.

The operating benefit may also be reduced by any amount reimbursed to the employer within 45 days of the calendar year end.

For capital cost allowance (CCA) purposes, the employer is restricted to $30,000 of the automobile cost on purchases made after 2000, not including federal and provincial sales tax. The annual CCA allowance is 30 per cent on a declining balance basis, except for the year of acquisition when the allowance is limited to one-half, or 15 per cent. Each car costing more than the allowable limit at the time of purchase is included in a separate CCA class with no recapture or terminal loss available upon disposal.

(A more complete description of CCA and how it works can be found on page 58).

The deduction for interest on money borrowed is restricted to a maximum of $300 per month if the automobile was purchased after 2000.

If the automobile is leased as per an agreement entered into after 2000, the maximum deduction is $800 per month (excluding PST and GST). This limit helps to ensure that the deduction level is consistent for both leased and purchased vehicles. Another restriction prorates deductible lease costs in situations where the value of the vehicle exceeds the CCA limit.

The employee benefit is generally calculated on the vehicle's full cost, regardless of the fact the employer is limited in the amount of capital cost, finance charges or lease payments they may write off for a passenger vehicle.

Note that some vehicles, such as those used for emergency response purposes (i.e., medical, fire or police), are not defined as automobiles for income tax purposes.

## Tax Tips

A standby charge may not apply under certain well-defined circumstances. If, for instance, the employer's policy is to have an employee return the automobile to company premises when they embark on a business trip, the standby charge should be prorated to exclude those days. But if the employee voluntarily leaves the automobile at the employer's premises over that period, those days will probably count toward the standby charge.

The full operating benefit for personal use of an automobile applies if the employer pays any operating expenses. Therefore, it may benefit you to fully reimburse your employer for such coverage.

The standby charge is calculated on the vehicle's original cost regardless of its age. If it is an older vehicle, consider purchasing the car from your employer. Note, however, that if a leased automobile is purchased at less than its fair market value, the difference is considered a taxable benefit and must be included in your income.

## Use of Employee-Owned Car

Employees who are required to travel on business or work away from their employer's office can use their own automobile. Employees required by terms of employment to provide their own vehicle, and who want to deduct the employment-related costs of operating the car, or any other employment-related expense (see Deductions from Employment Income, page 32), must file Form T2200. The employer must sign this form annually, certifying the required conditions were met during that year.

Employees who are required to pay their own automobile expenses are entitled to deduct business-related vehicle expenses that are not reimbursed by the employer. Deductions for the capital cost or lease cost of the vehicle are limited in their extent just as they are for employer-owned automobiles.

Deductions for expenses such as gasoline, insurance, maintenance, license, auto-club membership, leasing costs and interest on money borrowed to purchase the car are normally allowable in the same proportion as business to total kilometres driven during the year. Major accident repair costs, minus insurance proceeds or damage claims, are also fully deductible provided the vehicle was used for business, not personal purposes, at the time of the accident.

Travel between an employee's home and their employer's office is generally considered to constitute personal, rather than business, use of the automobile. In 2007, however, a taxpayer successfully appealed a CRA decision to disallow expense deductions incurred to and from the office on the grounds that their employer required them to have a car at work every day, thus preventing them from commuting using less expensive modes of transportation. Furthermore, if required to make a business stop between their home and office at the request of their employer, the entire distance travelled throughout the day may constitute business, rather than personal use.

Any proportion of an employer-paid automobile allowance that is deemed by the CRA to be unreasonably high is taxable to the employee. The maximum amount the employer may claim in 2008 has been established by the CRA at 52 cents per kilometre for the first 5,000 kilometres of business travel in a year (up from 50 cents in 2007) and 46 cents per kilometre thereafter (up from 44 cents in 2007).

For the Yukon Territory, Northwest Territories and Nunavut, the corresponding tax-exempt allowance is 56 cents per kilometre for the first 5,000 kilometres driven (up from 54 cents in 2007), and 50 cents for each kilometre thereafter (up from 48 cents in 2007).

Alternatively, an employee who receives an unreasonably low allowance may choose to include that amount in income and then deduct the actual business-use expenses. However, employees cannot refuse to accept a reasonable allowance without also jeopardizing their ability to claim a deduction for automobile expenses.

Employer-subsidized parking must generally be included in income if the benefit is being provided primarily to the employee. However, if the parking spot is provided for the primary benefit of the employer, to allow the employee to use their automobile in the course of carrying out business-related duties during office hours, or save on taxi fares when required to work late, all or a proportion of this amount might be reduced or waived.

An allowance based on anything other than actual business travel on a per-kilometre basis is not considered reasonable and must therefore be included in the employee's income. Similarly, should the actual expenses be reimbursed, any additional allowance would be considered unreasonable and need to be treated as income.

It is acceptable for an employer and employee to agree on a periodic advance based on a reasonable estimate of business kilometres driven. At the calendar year end or termination of employment, whichever comes first, the employee and employer must reconcile that advance against the actual distance traveled on behalf of the company. If the advance was inadequate the employer must make up the shortfall, whereas the employee must return any excess should the reverse situation occur. Once an employee receives a reasonable allowance to cover all employment-related use of their automobile, no further expenses can be claimed for tax purposes.

## Tax Tips

Special rules might apply for a van, pickup truck, or a similar vehicle (like a sport utility vehicle) used in the course of business, particularly where they involve travel to a remote or special work site. If you drive one of these vehicles to earn income, check with your Certified General Accountant to see which rules apply to you.

Keep a record log, in addition to relevant travel receipts, to support business mileage. Without a statistical record, taxpayers often have a tendency to overestimate the percentage of mileage incurred as a result of business activities.

If your employer allows you to keep an office in your home, but also requires that you travel to head office on business, related travel expense allowances have been ruled by the courts as being exempt from taxation.

Salespersons or other employees who live and travel in a motor home might be able to deduct expenses of that motor home relative to the proportion it is used for business (i.e., distance travelled).

If you have an arrangement with your employer that involves a combination of both a flat rate and per kilometre travel allowance for the same vehicle, the tax treatment might be complex, particularly if some automobile expenses were also reimbursed. Your Certified General Accountant can assist in this process.

## Loans to Employees

A loan or any other debt owed by an employee to their employer potentially creates an attributed taxable benefit based on the prescribed rate of interest set quarterly by the CRA. The employer must record any difference between the prescribed and actual interest rates as employment income on the employee's T4.

When borrowed funds are used to acquire either income-producing property or an automobile or aircraft for employment use, the interest amount actually paid or imputed may be deductible as an offsetting expense against the resulting investment or employment income.

The imputed benefit of a loan used for a home purchase or refinancing is calculated using the lesser of the prescribed rate in effect at the time the loan was made (refer to Appendix VII, page 217), or the prescribed rate for each quarterly period the loan remains outstanding. Employees will remain liable for this taxation benefit even if they transfer the home to a relative. All employee home-purchase loans are deemed to have a five-year maximum term, after which they are deemed to have been re-established at the prescribed rate in effect at that time.

An employee who receives a home relocation loan from an employer for a move designed to bring them at least 40 kilometres closer to their new place of business may be eligible to deduct attributed interest on up to $25,000 of loan principal for five years.

When the full or partial proceeds of a loan from an employer are forgiven, that amount is considered to be a taxable benefit to the employee.

The tax treatment on loans to employees might be less favourable if the employee is also a shareholder of the company making the loan.

## Tax Tips

Borrowing funds from your employer may prove to be more efficient and less expensive than other sources, even though you may pay tax on the imputed interest benefit. Note, however, that careful evaluation of borrowing alternatives may require professional advice.

If you expect interest rates to increase, consider renegotiating an employee home-purchase loan for an additional term. If you have predicted correctly, the taxable benefit might be minimized over the next five years of that term.

## Retiring Allowance and Termination Payments

A retiring allowance, including termination damages, paid to an employee upon or after retirement to recognize long service or to compensate for office or employment loss, must be included in income. Retirement refers to retirement from an employer, regardless of whether the employee is of normal retirement age. If the employee receives the allowance in instalments, they are taxable in the year received.

The employer is not required to withhold tax if the tax eligible retiring allowance is contributed directly to the employee's registered retirement savings plan (RRSP). Otherwise, if the employee receives the payment directly, tax must be withheld. Employees may then contribute to their plan up to 60 days after the year of receipt, claim that amount as a deduction on their tax return and recover the corresponding tax withheld.

In addition to an individual's normal RRSP contribution limits, retiring allowances transferred to an RRSP are allowable to a maximum of $2,000 for each employment year prior to 1996, plus an additional $1,500 for each employment year prior to 1989 in which the employee did not have vested rights in an employer-sponsored pension plan at retirement.

Years of past service need not have been continuous. Where there were gaps in employment and the employee has "bought back" years of service under a registered pension plan, special taxation rules may apply.

The fair market value of any benefit received by an employee in recognition of their long service will also likely qualify as a retiring allowance under the *Income Tax Act*. If, for instance, an employer buys out an automobile lease on behalf of an employee at a discount from fair market value, any resulting taxable benefit could qualify as a retiring allowance.

The payment of accumulated sick leave credits may also qualify as a retiring allowance if such payment is made in recognition of long service or in respect of the loss of an office or employment.

The fair market value of other property, such as shares, jewellery or life insurance policies, which are not paid for, but instead received in respect of a loss of office or employment, may also be considered part of an employee's retiring allowance, and therefore included in their income.

All or a portion of payments with respect to a loss of employment may still qualify as a retiring allowance, even if they are made before the employer/employee relationship has been formally severed. If, however, a retiring allowance initiates while an employee remains on the company's payroll, there must be some evidence the cessation of that relationship, including the receipt of individual employee benefits (i.e., they don't also extend to other former employees), is scheduled to occur at a fixed date.

The CRA stated in 2006 that if, following retirement, an employee is rehired by the same employer, or by an affiliated, non-arm's-length company pursuant to an arrangement made prior to retirement, they would generally not qualify for a retiring allowance. However, it also identified certain exceptions where the retirement allowance might not be adversely affected, such as when a retired civil servant subsequently obtains part-time employment in a different area of government, without any continuation of pension benefits, solely through their own efforts. Such cases will be examined on an individual basis.

Taxpayers who receive a retroactive lump-sum payment of at least $3,000 as part of a lump-sum settlement related to dismissal from an office or employment (or other qualifying award) may qualify for federal tax relief. A mechanism exists to provide such taxpayers with the opportunity to deduct any excess tax liability that may result from declaring settlement proceeds all at once as they must do under the current system, rather than being able to apply it retroactively to the respective year(s) related to the settlement.

---

### Tax Tips

Employees who retire but retain a seat on the board of directors of a private company at nominal compensation might still be eligible to collect a retiring allowance.

In cases involving a loss of office or employment, you may receive an amount awarded as damages by a human rights tribunal. If that amount is part of a retiring allowance, you might be able to exclude a reasonable amount of such an allowance from income for tax purposes.

A severance amount paid to a spouse or common-law partner as a result of working in a family business such as farming may qualify as a retiring allowance regardless of past remuneration, provided an employer/employee relationship existed over that period and the proposed retiring allowance is considered reasonable by the CRA.

---

## Retirement Compensation Arrangement

A retirement compensation arrangement (RCA) might be established under which the taxpayer's current or former employer, or another non-arm's-length party, has contributed funds. Such payments, made prior to retirement or the loss of an office, would be designed to fund future payments in case the taxpayer vacates that office. The RCA may provide for discretionary payments prior to the loss of such office if the taxpayer can prove there has been a "substantial change" in the services required.

Examples of a substantial change in duties may include situations such as where a former officer of a company is retained as a consultant, or a professional athlete resigns as a player but continues to provide services to the sporting franchise as a member of the coaching staff or as a scout.

RCA plans are very specific and do not overlap with other plans such as a deferred profit sharing plan, employee profit sharing plan or employee trust, among others. Consult your local Certified General Accountant for details.

## Legal Expenses Incurred

Taxpayers can deduct legal expenses incurred and paid during the year to obtain a pension benefit or retiring allowance in respect of employment. In any single year this deduction is limited to the pension or retiring allowance received, less any related transfer to an RRSP or RPP.

Expenses that are not deductible in a particular year may be carried forward seven years.

A separate provision of the *Income Tax Act* allows individuals to deduct legal costs paid to collect salary or wages. Even if they are never collected, a deduction is allowed provided the employee incurs costs to establish a right to wages or salary.

Legal expenses associated with establishing a right to collect salary or wages may be incurred from a variety of sources, including for example, a former or current employer, or a professional association.

In a related matter, it used to be the long-standing administrative practice of the CRA not to tax prejudgment interest on awards with respect to wrongful dismissal. However, that policy changed in 2004 and prejudgment interest relating to wrongful dismissal is now taxable. Check with your Certified General Accountant to determine the correct tax treatment if this situation applies to you.

## Tax Tips

Legal fees incurred in a termination case don't necessarily have to be paid to a lawyer in order to be deductible. Fees paid to another professional, such as a labour relations consultant retained to negotiate a severance package, may also be deductible.

## Death Benefits

When an employee dies and an employer makes a payment to the surviving spouse or common-law partner or other beneficiary in recognition of the deceased's employment, the first $10,000 of this amount is generally a tax-free death benefit.

This $10,000 exemption first applies to the surviving spouse or common-law partner. If the surviving spouse or common-law partner receives less than $10,000, and other beneficiaries are entitled to receive a benefit in respect of the employee, their exempt limit will be $10,000, less any amount already claimed by the surviving spouse. The remaining exempt portion would then be shared on a pro-rata basis among the other beneficiaries.

From a tax point of view, it is possible to have more than one spouse or common-law partner (e.g., a legally married spouse and a common-law partner). If more than one spouse or common-law partner is entitled to receive a death benefit with respect to a deceased individual, the resulting benefit must be allocated on a pro-rata basis.

# INCOME AND DIVIDENDS FROM A BUSINESS AND SELF-EMPLOYMENT

Self-employed individuals, unlike those who are employed by others, have the right to control a number of factors in their work environment, such as the hiring and firing of staff, wages or salary to be paid and the place and manner in which work is done. They are also responsible for supplying the tools of their trade along with covering overhead and other expenses.

A measure of uncertainty arises with that control. Generally speaking, self-employed individuals, unlike employees, have no guarantee of a steady income because their remuneration depends on the continuing success of their business enterprise; thus, there is a greater degree of financial risk.

CRA Guide RC4110, entitled *Employee or Self-Employed?* outlines detailed criteria for determining whether a taxpayer is employed or self-employed. The major themes of this booklet include an analysis of who has control over the working environment and time spent on the job;

who owns the tools and equipment necessary to do the job; as well as who bears the brunt of responsibility for a potential risk/reward scenario when it comes to a financial profit or loss.

Determining whether an individual should be classified as self-employed or as an employee for tax purposes is sometimes complicated. Your Certified General Accountant can assist in making this determination.

### Tax Tips

Self-employment might also exist in circumstances where a worker is hired through an agency for various temporary assignments.

## Accounting for Business Income

With the exception of farmers and fishers, self-employed taxpayers must generally declare income in the period it is earned, even if the remuneration billed for is collected in a subsequent period. Expenses incurred to earn that revenue must be matched in the same period, even if they are paid in a subsequent time frame. This is known as the accrual method of accounting.

Under accrual accounting, for instance, construction contractors would normally declare any progress billings made, less amounts withheld pending satisfactory completion of a job, as earned income for that period. However, contractors may also elect to include such holdbacks in their income for that year, provided they administer the same accounting treatment to all contracts.

The correct tax treatment to apply in specific instances could differ. Your Certified General Accountant can assist you in this area.

## Royalty Income

Royalty income, such as that received by an author or musician, is generally considered to be investment income, although it might also be classified under some circumstances as business or employment income.

Because the tax treatment for royalty income can be complicated, it is best to check with your Certified General Accountant to determine the correct tax treatment to apply towards it.

## Salary versus Dividends

To maximize the availability of after-tax funds and minimize total corporate and personal tax, an owner/manager should consider the appropriate mix of salary and dividends to receive as compensation.

Although the tax system is designed to extract approximately the same combined corporate and personal tax dollars regardless of any salary and dividend mix, perfect integration does not always occur.

No two situations are identical and the optimum combination of salary and dividends can only be determined on an individual basis. However, the following factors should be considered:

- whether tax credits or losses are available to reduce corporate tax otherwise payable, in which case dividends may be preferable to salary;

- dividends can be received tax-free to the extent the company has a balance in its capital dividend account;

- dividends may trigger refundable taxes to the corporation, resulting in a reduction of taxes payable;

- dividends may reduce the individual's cumulative net investment loss (CNIL) account;

- dividends, when taken with other tax preference items, may result in alternative minimum tax (AMT). Sufficient salary or bonus may eliminate or reduce AMT;

- salary or bonus in the current year creates earned income necessary for RRSP contributions in the subsequent year whereas dividends do not;

- share redemption or reduction of shareholder advances to a corporation as an alternative to paying either dividends and/or salary can result in a tax-free return of paid-up capital or debt;

- the existence of payroll-related costs, such as employment insurance (if the shareholder owns 40 per cent or less of the company) and Canada Pension Plan (CPP) premiums. However, dividends are not used for the calculation of CPP and Employment Insurance (EI); and

- there is a federal small business deduction of 16 per cent on the active business income of Canadian-controlled private corporations (CCPC) for up to $400,000. Most provinces and territories also have special rates and thresholds for small businesses in their jurisdictions.

## Related Issues Affecting Business Income and Dividends

# Establishing a Management Company or Professional Corporation

There may be certain tax advantages associated with establishing a management company to provide non-professional services or products to a professional at a reasonable mark-up (e.g., the CRA generally considers 15 per cent to be reasonable in many instances).

If incorporated by a professional's spouse or common-law partner, for example, a management company can be used to split income in addition to providing other incorporation benefits, such as a tax deferral. As earnings are taxed at the lower corporate tax rate, more cash may be available for working capital or the purchase of capital assets.

Those in charge of establishing management companies should ensure they are not deemed to be personal services businesses. A personal services business is defined by the *Income Tax Act* as a corporation through which an individual delivers services to a recipient individual, partnership or organization, etc., which he or she would otherwise be considered an officer or employee of. As a means of discouraging individuals from providing such services through a corporation, personal services businesses are denied the small business deduction as well as being limited in terms of eligible expense deductions.

This restriction could, for instance, apply to a business that does not have more than five full-time employees (although additional part-time employees might be enough to qualify it for a deduction, according to a 2008 court ruling).

The Goods and Services Tax (GST) also reduces some of the potential advantages for exempt professionals to establish management companies. For instance, while management companies must charge GST on fees and mark-ups, the exempt practitioner is unable to recover the GST as an input credit.

Some provinces allow certain professionals to form professional corporations. Note, however, that there are legal differences between management companies and professional corporations. Furthermore, professional corporations face certain restrictions compared to other corporations.

Check with your Certified General Accountant and lawyer to make sure you understand all the taxation, legal and other important aspects that apply to your circumstances before taking any action with respect to incorporation.

## Business Partnership

Various business partnerships may exist between two or more people. The agreement between these business principals is likely to cover a multitude of issues, including the distribution of subsequent profits and losses, which could be equal or in some other proportion reflecting the degree of their involvement in the business; the initial financial investment; proportion of risk assumed; or other criteria.

In addition to an arm's-length partnership, it may also be possible for the owner of an unincorporated business to establish their spouse or common-law partner as a partner who is eligible to share in the business's profits or losses. To qualify as a partner, the spouse or common-law partner will be required to:

- contribute a significant amount of time, specified skill or training to the business; or
- invest property in the business.

The allocation of partnership income or losses should be reasonable under the circumstances. Partners should be aware that a provision of the *Income Tax Act* allows the CRA to reallocate income or losses among the partners if it is determined that the primary motivation for selecting a particular allocation is to reduce or postpone tax that would otherwise be payable.

Special rules apply to limited partnerships. Consult your Certified General Accountant for details.

## Share Structure

Owner/managers often hold corporate shares in a CCPC. It is also possible for an individual to own shares of a holding company, which in turn owns all the shares of the operating company. Under this structure, dividends may be passed tax free among CCPCs. By doing this, funds can be transferred away from future risks associated with the operating company without incurring additional income taxes. Provided excess funds are not personally required, this might be advantageous in certain situations.

Although investment capital accumulation in the holding company may cause complications with respect to claiming the small business corporation (SBC) capital gains deduction on a subsequent sale of shares, this potential problem can generally be remedied if appropriate steps are taken prior to disposition. You might want to discuss this with your Certified General Accountant.

In determining whether a corporation qualifies as a CCPC, it is important to ascertain not just the current share ownership, but also with whom the right of control resides. If, for instance, a foreign-based minority owner has the right to either acquire shares or dilute ownership such that the company is no longer majority owned by Canadian parties, it could be denied status as a CCPC.

The size of the business may also be a factor; for example, if it does not have more than five full-time employees it might be considered a specified investment business and, therefore, not qualify for the small business deduction.

Share restructuring can also be conducive towards establishing a potential estate freeze. A capital gain realized on the ultimate sale of qualifying small business shares might, for instance, be split among several family members holding shares, each with an available $750,000 lifetime capital gains deduction (see Capital Gains Deduction on page 73 for a discussion of the conditions that qualify).

Decisions handed down in several recent court cases have reinforced that family members are eligible to receive dividends regardless of the degree of their participation in helping to establish or run a family business.

## Loans to Shareholders

Generally, a shareholder loan is required to be included in the taxpayer's income in the year the loan is made. However, there are certain exceptions. One is that the loan must be repaid by the end of the following fiscal year of the corporation making the loan, provided it is not part of a series of loans and repayments.

The imposition of taxable benefits on a shareholder loan is based on prescribed interest rates, as applied to the loan principal outstanding. Loan repayments are applied to outstanding balances on a first in, first out basis. The payment of dividends, salaries and bonuses may also qualify as legitimate repayments of a shareholder loan, provided that amount is included in the taxpayer's income.

If bona-fide arrangements were made when the loan originated that repayment would take place within a reasonable period of time, that loan might not be considered income if it occurred in the ordinary course of the lender's business or was made to enable a shareholder who is also an employee that deals at arm's length with the corporation to:

- acquire a dwelling for their own use; or
- purchase an automobile for use in the course of employment; or
- purchase fully paid shares from the corporation or a related corporation (provided such shares are held by the individuals for their own benefit).

## Preserving Business Losses

A business with non-capital loss carryovers that are due to expire may increase taxable income, in order to use as much of the loss as possible, by any of the following methods:

- reduce CCA claims and amortization of eligible capital expenditures (see section on page 58);
- compensate employee shareholders by declaring dividends rather than pay a salary (assuming there are sufficient retained earnings);
- sell redundant fixed assets or other capital property when this will result in a recapture of CCA;

- reduce tax reserves, including reserves for doubtful accounts;
- elect to capitalize interest and related costs on money borrowed to acquire depreciable property;
- transfer losses to another corporation within the corporate group as losses may be used within that group by means of an amalgamation or wind-up, subject to restrictions if a change of control results;
- value the business inventory at FMV. Note, however, that a change in the method of valuing inventory must result in a more appropriate way of calculating income. The Minister of National Revenue must also approve this change;
- realize capital gains on investments;
- bring capital gains reserves into income; or
- apply losses to a corporation's part IV account (referred to in the *Income Tax Act* as tax on taxable dividends received by private corporations), if no other alternative is viable.

## Choice of Year End

### Proprietorship/Partnership

All sole proprietorships, professional corporations that are partnership members and partnerships (where at least one member is an individual, professional corporation or other affected partnership) are generally required to have a December 31 fiscal year end.

If an appropriate election is made, however, some businesses may qualify to establish an alternative fiscal year end and estimate calendar-year business income using a specified formula. The alternative method is a one-time election that must be made by the taxpayer (or, in the case of a partnership, by a representative on behalf of all members). This election must be made by the filing due date of the first tax return that includes the business's income.

The alternative method election remains in effect until it is revoked or the business no longer qualifies to apply it. Once a December 31 year end is used for tax reporting, however, the business cannot subsequently elect to use the alternative method.

In the year an individual dies, goes bankrupt or otherwise ceases to carry on the business, there can be no additional income inclusion under the alternative method unless, in the case of business cessation, a similar business is started in the same calendar year.

Some taxpayers in a partnership arrangement are required to fill out CRA Form T5013 — *Statement of Partnership Income.*

The rules governing this subject are complex. Taxpayers are advised to consult a Certified General Accountant for more details.

## Corporation

A corporation can choose its first year end, which must be within 53 weeks from the date of incorporation.

In establishing an incorporated business's fiscal period, the timing of income recognition is often a major consideration although other factors, such as the normal business cycle, should also be weighed into the decision.

# BUSINESS AND SELF-EMPLOYMENT EXPENSES

Individuals may deduct all expenses incurred in the conduct of their business, provided they are undertaken to earn income, are reasonable under the circumstances and not limited or prohibited by certain rules or regulations established with respect to specific expenses.

Examples of business expenses may include all or part of the following:

- accounting;
- advertising;
- amortization of capital assets;
- bad debts;
- business-related memberships and subscriptions;
- business-related start-up costs;
- business taxes, fees and dues;
- certain group benefits;

- collection (i.e., related to bad debt);
- convention expenses (up to two a year);
- consulting;
- delivery and freight;
- disability-related modification expenses;
- equipment rental;
- insurance (fire, theft, liability);
- interest and bank charges;
- legal;
- light, heat and water;
- maintenance and repairs (other than for passenger motor vehicles);
- management and administration fees;
- meals and entertainment expenses;
- motor vehicle expenses (such as fuel, insurance and repairs);
- office expenses (including postage, stationery, telephone and other supplies);
- property taxes or rent on business property;
- purchases of materials and supplies;
- representation costs to obtain a business-related licence, permit, franchise or trademark;
- salaries and amounts paid "in kind";
- specific courses taken to improve business skills;
- subcontractors' costs;
- travelling expenses (limitations apply to motor vehicles); and
- workspace in the home (when appropriate).

## Tax Tips

Self-employment expenses must be documented. There are instances where the tax courts have disallowed what might otherwise have been legitimate expenses because of poor or non-existent documentation. A lack of proof to support the taxpayer's argument in the event of a dispute with the CRA could also lead to the imposition, or upholding, of penalties.

## Other Deductions

Individuals who are self-employed can deduct the employer's share of Canada Pension Plan (CPP) and Quebec Pension Plan (QPP) earned income contributions. They can also deduct premiums paid for coverage under a provincial worker's compensation board, such as the Workplace Safety and Insurance Board (WSIB) in Ontario.

Self-employed individuals may also, within limits, deduct health and dental premiums paid on behalf of them or immediate family members sustained under a private health services plan (PHSP), provided they are actively engaged in the business and derive more than 50 per cent of their income from it.

## Legitimacy of Expense Deductions

When determining whether a self-employment enterprise, such as a sole proprietorship or partnership, constitutes a true business with allowable expense deductions, the tax courts generally place a great deal of emphasis on determining the commercial viability of the enterprise.

Hence, the taxpayer must establish that his or her prominent intention is to make a profit and, in so doing, they are employing objective standards in their conduct of the business.

The courts will also look at factors such as the amount of time and capital devoted to the business, the existence of a solid business plan, whether or not there is adequate capitalization, ties to professional associations, the training of its entrepreneur(s) and, depending on the nature of the enterprise, the existence of employees.

If there is a personal element associated with the business operation (i.e., if it has been established as a hobby), the expenses associated with that personal element are likely to be denied as taxable deductions. The Tax Court might then turn its attention toward determining whether or not the activity was also being carried out in a sufficiently commercial manner as to constitute a source of income, in which case a proportion of its expenses might be related to commercial operations and therefore be deductible. Somebody utilizing their artistic talents such as painting, writing or photography in a business endeavour should, for example, be especially diligent about being able to provide tangible proof their enterprise is predominantly commercial in nature.

One of the tests the courts are likely to employ in this situation is a determination regarding whether or not the business was established with, and maintains, a reasonable expectation of profit (REOP) within a reasonable period of time.

## Deductions Related to Salary Paid to Spouse/Common-Law Partner or Children

If a spouse, common-law partner or other family member is employed by a business, whether it be incorporated, a partnership or sole proprietorship, there are potential opportunities for income splitting and reduction of the family's overall tax burden.

The following criteria must be met if a business is to be allowed a deduction for salary paid to a family member:

- the salary must be paid periodically, preferably by cheque for bona-fide services performed;
- an employer-employee relationship must exist; and
- any salary paid must be reasonable for the work performed.

Normal payroll deductions apply for non-arm's-length employees (such as a spouse or child), except for employment insurance (EI) premiums which may be exempt. Consult your Certified General Accountant with the particulars of your situation.

### Tax Tips

The salary paid to a family member may allow that individual to become eligible for CPP and RRSP contributions.

You should be especially vigilant about documenting the work carried out by family members in order to help prove the compensation they received was equitable.

## Deductions Related to Workspace in the Home

The *Income Tax Act* limits the circumstances under which a self-employed individual can deduct the costs related to a workspace in the home. They are confined to situations where the space is used exclusively to earn income from a business and on a regular and continuous basis for meeting clients, customers or patients, or it is the individual's principal place of business.

This claim may be based on the proportionate space within the home that is used as a workplace. Eligible expenses include rent, mortgage interest, realty taxes, insurance, utilities and maintenance. It is generally not advisable to claim capital cost allowance (CCA) (see page 58) on a portion of the home because that portion would then not qualify for the principal residence exemption when it is ultimately sold.

Similarly, claiming 50 per cent or more business use of the home or making major structural alterations to adapt it to business use, will trigger a "change in use" resulting in loss of the principal residence exemption.

The amount a taxpayer can claim is limited to their business income before deductions for home workspace. Any unused amount may then be carried forward and claimed in the subsequent year against related business income. To the extent that unused amounts cannot be claimed in the following year, they can be carried forward indefinitely to be claimed at the first available opportunity.

---

**Tax Tips**

Don't forget to include business storage space in the basement and elsewhere, when determining the proportion of your home used for commercial purposes.

A bed and breakfast enterprise may also qualify as workspace in the home, provided the guest rooms are located inside the owner's home and not in a separate dwelling.

---

## Automobile Expenses

The *Income Tax Act* restricts certain expenses relating to "passenger vehicles." A passenger vehicle, which can include a van, pickup truck or sport utility vehicle, is defined as a motor vehicle designed to carry no more than nine persons, including a driver and luggage. It does not fit this definition if:

- 90 per cent or more of its use is for the transportation of goods, equipment or passengers in the course of income-earning activities; or
- more than 50 per cent of its use is for such activities and it seats not more than three people, including the driver.

The restrictions on deductible expenses and related business use calculations are both discussed under Use of Company Cars, on page 35.

It is impossible to provide a simple rule of thumb with respect to an automobile lease versus purchase decision. Each situation must be carefully reviewed and many factors, including interest rates, mileage allowances and expected resale value, plus income tax implications, taken into consideration before a final decision is made. Certified General Accountants are well equipped to help in this process.

## Deduction for Business Meals and Entertainment

The *Income Tax Act* imposes a restriction on the deductibility of business-related meals, beverages and entertainment expenses, based on a general presumption that these normally combine elements of both a personal and business nature. Only 50 per cent of such expenses are deductible — with certain exceptions, such as when employees are required to work at selected special work sites or in remote locations; are travelling aboard an airplane, train or bus on business; or they are incurred at a fundraising event to benefit a registered charity, among others.

The 2007 federal budget increased this allowance to 80 per cent for long-haul truck drivers while they are working. This increase will be phased in over a five-year period. It was 60 per cent for expenses incurred on or after March 19, 2007; that allowance increased to 65 per cent on January 1, 2008.

The 50 per cent rule also applies to meals and entertainment provided as part of a convention, seminar or similar event, where the organizer may specify a reasonable amount to cover the cost of food and entertainment. Otherwise, the fee for that event will be deemed to include $50 a day for meals and/or entertainment. (Incidental refreshments, such as coffee and doughnuts, are exempt from this calculation.) Certain other expenses, such as transportation costs incurred to get people to attend an entertainment event, might also be subject to this 50 per cent restriction.

Bottles of liquor or certain food items given as gifts at Christmas or on other special occasions may also fall within the auspices of this 50 per cent limitation. However, some food, beverage and entertainment-related expenses for up to six special events in a calendar year, such as Christmas parties and employee meetings, held at a particular place of business to which all of the firm's employees are invited, might be 100 per cent deductible. Business owners with employees should therefore consult their Certified General Accountant for a clarification of these rules.

## Capital Cost Allowance (CCA)

Capital assets such as land, buildings, automobiles, furniture, computers, etc., provide an enduring benefit to a business. This period is generally recognized by the accounting profession as being at least one year; in practice, most capital assets provide benefits that last for several years. Capital costs also include items such as legal, accounting and other professional fees paid to acquire the property.

Individuals who run their own business cannot therefore expense, or write off the cost of such assets immediately upon purchase; rather, they must spread the cost over several years. For tax purposes, this write-off is referred to as capital cost allowance (CCA) and it is subject to strict rules and limitations. Assets are grouped into approximately 40 classes where items are provided with a discretionary allowance claimed annually at a fixed percentage, generally on a declining balance basis.

A small sampling of common CCA classes, a description of what is contained in those classes, and their corresponding deduction rates include:

- automobile (class 10 or 10.1) 30 per cent on a declining balance basis;
- computer software (class 12) 100 per cent on a declining balance basis;
- furniture and fixtures (class 8) 20 per cent on a declining balance basis;
- manufacturing and processing machinery (class 43) 30 per cent on a declining balance basis;
- leasehold improvements, which may either be written off on a straight-line basis over the term of the lease (including the first renewal period), or five years, whichever is greater.

Special rules apply for class 10.1 automobiles, the cost of which exceeds the threshold amount of $30,000 prior to sales taxes.

Special rates also apply to computer equipment. The federal budget in 2004 increased the CCA rate on such items acquired after March 22, 2004, to 45 per cent from 30 per cent. The federal budget in 2007 further increased the CCA rate on such items acquired on or after March 19, 2007, to 55 per cent from 45 per cent.

The rates for broadband, Internet and other data-network infrastructure equipment were increased to 30 per cent from 20 per cent in 2004.

New CCA classes have also been created to accommodate equipment qualifying for these accelerated rates.

In most cases, only one-half of the normal allowance is available on depreciable property acquired in an arm's-length transaction in the fiscal period it is acquired. Where the fiscal period is less than 365 days the amount that would otherwise be claimed must be prorated, based on the number of days in that period.

The 2007 federal budget established a temporary two-year 50 per cent straight line accelerated CCA rate to cover investment in manufacturing or processing machinery and equipment undertaken prior to 2009, as an economic incentive to Canada's manufacturing sector.

Budget 2008 extended this by three years until the end of 2011. However, the straight line depreciation will only continue to apply to eligible assets purchased in 2009. Eligible assets purchased in 2010 will be subject to a 50 per cent declining balance rate that year, followed by a 40 per cent declining balance write-off in 2011, and 30 per cent thereafter.

Eligible assets acquired in 2011 will be allowed a 40 per cent declining balance write-off that year only; then 30 per cent thereafter.

Certain types of equipment can become obsolete before being fully depreciated for income tax purposes. Taxpayers may elect to place eligible rapidly depreciating equipment in a separate class. Examples of eligible property include certain computers, photocopiers, fax machines or telephone equipment costing more than $1,000. If such property has not been disposed of after five years, it must be transferred to the general class to which it would have originally been placed.

A terminal loss could result on the disposition of such elected property should the proceeds ultimately received be less than any remaining undepreciated capital cost (UCC). Consult your Certified General Accountant for details on these and other specific rules, such as the correct tax treatment associated with any subsequent recapture of CCA, as well as a full clarification of CCA classes and the multitude of items contained within.

---

### Tax Tips

If you dispose of one of several identical eligible capital properties with a shared value, you may use an average cost to determine the value of the individual property sold.

Specific costs incurred by employers to improve business premises access for people with disabilities may be deducted in the year they are incurred and need not be capitalized.

You do not have to claim all eligible CCA amounts in the year they are incurred if you believe it may be tax advantageous to carry all, or some, of that amount forward to a future year.

---

## Eligible Capital Expenditures and Receipts

Certain expenditures are capital in nature, but not included in any CCA class that qualifies them to be written off on a declining balance basis. These include, but are not limited to, expenditures related to acquiring certain government rights, trademarks, franchises, incorporation fees, certain farm-related quotas and goodwill.

Seventy-five per cent of such expenditures may be amortized at a rate of 7 per cent per year on a declining balance basis.

When this type of capital asset is sold, income is generated when applied to the recapture of depreciation amounts previously written off, with any remainder treated as a taxable capital gain from a capital property disposition. Such a sale could also generate a loss, in which case special rules apply.

Consult your Certified General Accountant for details.

## Input Tax Credit

The Input Tax Credit is a credit, or refund, claimed by registrants on goods and services tax (GST) and harmonized sales tax (HST) returns (for the provinces of New Brunswick, Nova Scotia and Newfoundland and Labrador) filed on a monthly, quarterly or annual basis. This credit covers GST/HST paid or payable in the course of any business activity.

The following criteria must be met in order for taxpayers to be eligible to claim the Input Tax Credit:

- the person making the claim must be registered;
- the registrant must deal with taxable supplies;
- goods or services must be acquired or imported for consumption, use or supply in the course of a commercial activity; and
- documentation pertaining to the tax paid or payable must be retained.

Consult your Certified General Accountant for details about the calculation methods available for you to claim this credit, the due dates for making this claim and other related information.

# FARMING INCOME/LOSSES AND OTHER SPECIAL CONSIDERATIONS

Farming is a very diverse and specialized industry in Canada. It encompasses a wide range of activities, including tilling the soil, livestock raising or showing, poultry raising, dairy farming, winery-related vineyard operations, tree farming, beekeeping and, in some instances, activities associated with raising fish, such as commercial shellfish, among others.

## Determining Whether Farming Constitutes the Main Source of Income

Qualified farm property (QFP) is defined in the *Income Tax Act* as property that is owned by the taxpayer, their spouse or common-law partner, or in a partnership, that was used "in the course of carrying on the business of farming in Canada" under some very specific scenarios.

The CRA may take several factors into consideration when determining whether taxpayers engage in farming activities to the extent that it constitutes their chief source of income. Taxpayers for whom farming does not represent their main source of income will be limited in their ability to deduct farm-related expenses.

The criteria used by the CRA to examine this issue include:

- whether or not the farming operation has a reasonable expectation of profit (REOP);
- whether earned profits from farming are substantial compared to the taxpayer's major source of income;
- whether there is a family history of farming activities;
- the extent of the taxpayer's knowledge of farming;
- whether the activity generating the taxpayer's major source of income has, to some degree, been subordinated as a result of farming activities; and
- the professionalism of business activities, including the existence of a business plan and the amount of time and capital committed.

Consult your Certified General Accountant for details.

## Method of Accounting

To accommodate myriad farming-related operations, there are a number of accounting and income tax provisions available.

Farmers and fishers have the option of reporting income using the cash (rather than the accrual) method of accounting. The cash method can be advantageous to farmers because it allows them to decide when to report income by timing the sale of produce or livestock in the most appropriate year. Using the cash method, farmers can also time expenses by paying accounts in the year they wish to make the deduction.

This timing option, which is not available to members of any other industry, can greatly increase tax-planning alternatives for the farming community.

Several additional calculations in determining farming income may also differ from those of other businesses. For instance, under the cash method of accounting, expenses relating to a taxation year that falls two or more years after the actual payment are not allowed as deductions in the current taxation year. If, for example, in December 2008 a farmer pays insurance premiums covering 2008, 2009 and 2010, the amount deductible on their 2008 income tax return would be limited to the actual cost of insurance for 2008 and 2009 only. Costs related to 2010 will only be deductible during 2010. Also, a farmer who enters into a three or more year equipment lease cannot deduct the portions that relate to lease payments beyond one year into the future — i.e., if the lease was signed in 2008, that would cover up until the end of 2009.

Tilling, clearing and levelling of farmland, as well as the building of an unpaved road, can be expensed in the year such payments are made or any portion carried forward to future years. However, land improvements on farmland rented out to another producer do not qualify for this deferral. In such cases, land improvements can be expensed in the current year or alternatively added to the cost of the land.

If the farmer is actively involved in peripheral activities, such as the purchase and sale of seed, this business is not considered farming and must be reported using the accrual method of accounting, which will include the reflection of inventories on hand at year end. The CRA will consider certain non-farming activities to be part of the farming operation if these activities are undertaken on a small scale and the income from them is incidental to other farming revenue.

Other differences that affect the farming industry include:

- assets purchased during the year are restricted by the CCA half-year rule, except assets such as quotas (which are eligible capital property), where the full amortization amount is allowed in the year of acquisition;

- deceased farmers' "rights and things" include harvested crops, livestock on hand (less the basic herd), supplies on hand, inventory and receivables (if the deceased used the cash basis of accounting); and

- no GST is charged on sales of most farm commodities. Registered farmers must, however, charge GST on items such as land and quota rentals and firewood sales that do not fall under the exception list provided by the CRA. Asset purchases and sales specifically exempt include tractors over 44.74 kW (60 PTO hp) and most harvesting, tillage, haying and grain-handling equipment. Consult the CRA list for further details.

Farmers and fishers should also be aware that:

- payments received out of the Agricultural Income Disaster Assistance (AIDA) and the Canadian Agriculture Income Stabilization (CAIS) programs are taxable when received;

- advance payments for a crop are considered to be a sale of that crop and are therefore taxable when received. However, advances under the Agricultural Marketing Program Act (AMPA) are considered loans and are not taxable when received. In this case, income is triggered when the crop is sold and the loan re-paid; and

- a farmer who plants an orchard must capitalize the cost of the trees by adding it to the adjusted cost base (ACB) of the land. Therefore, those trees would not qualify for capital cost allowance (CCA). However, replacement trees can be expensed in the current year.

## Tax Tips

If you are a farmer using the cash method of accounting, note that when an expense is paid using a credit card, the relevant date for tax purposes occurs when the expense is charged to the credit card, not when the credit card is paid.

Expenses for dogs and cats located on the farm are deductible if those expenses relate to their use for rodent or other wild animal control.

## Mandatory Inventory Adjustment (MIA)

Whenever cash basis accounting results in a farming loss, a mandatory inventory adjustment (MIA) must be performed with respect to purchased inventory on hand at year end. The MIA is calculated by adding to income the lesser of the loss amount and FMV of the purchased inventory, such as livestock, feed, fertilizer, fuel and other supplies on hand.

For MIA purposes, inventory is generally valued at the lower of its original purchase price and FMV. Specified animals are valued at their original purchase price, less 30 per cent per annum on a diminishing balance basis, unless the taxpayer elects to value them at a greater amount that does not exceed their original cost. All horses are specified animals; cattle registered under the *Livestock Pedigree Act* may also be treated as specified animals at the taxpayer's option.

## Optional Inventory Adjustment (OIA)

Farmers can elect to report an optional inventory adjustment (OIA) at year end to help reduce wide swings in net income that sometimes occur under the cash basis of accounting. The OIA is calculated on an individual, rather than a partnership, basis.

Using the OIA, the taxpayer may elect to decrease expenses by an amount up to the full FMV of inventory on hand at year end. The OIA claimed in one year then becomes an increase in expenses the following year.

## Restricted Losses

Taxpayers who are engaged in farming activities, but for whom farming is not deemed by the CRA to be their "chief source of income" — either by itself or in combination with some other economic activity — may be restricted in any loss they can claim against other income. Recent court cases appear to be taking a more liberal approach as to whether farming, in combination with some another endeavour of the taxpayer, represents a major source of income.

That claim is limited to the first $2,500 of farm losses, plus one-half of the next $12,500 of such losses, for a maximum claim of $8,750 in one year. Any loss in excess of that claim is identified as a "restricted farm loss" which can be carried back up to three years, or forward up to 20 years for losses incurred and credits earned in taxation years that end after 2005 (up from 10 years previously as announced in the 2006 federal budget), and applied against farming income.

(The same carryback and carryforward provisions pertain to regular farm losses.)

Farmers cannot use restricted farm losses to create or increase a capital loss on the sale of farmland. However, any portion of outstanding restricted farm losses may be added to the adjusted cost base (ACB) of farm property in order to reduce the capital gain realized upon disposition. The allowable portion of such losses applied is limited to the property taxes and interest on money borrowed to purchase land.

A full-time farmer who has to take a part-time outside job to support the farm should be able to claim all their farm losses for tax purposes without application of the restricted farm loss rules.

## Investment Tax Credit Related to Farming Operations

A Scientific Research and Experimental Development (SR&ED) investment tax credit (ITC) may be claimed on that portion of the farmer's "checkoff," "assessment" or "levy" — terms that are used for determining eligibility for the SR&ED by the commodity boards.

Individuals qualify for a 20 per cent investment tax credit on the amount that is considered applicable to SR&ED expenditures by, for example, the wheat and corn boards. The boards then usually issue a statement or letter to the producer identifying the proper amount to claim.

Individuals claiming this ITC must fill out CRA Form T2038.

## Farm Dispositions and Capital Gains

Farm property dispositions may qualify for the $750,000 lifetime capital gains exemption available (up from $500,000 effective March 19, 2007), subject to certain restrictions. If, for example, the farm was purchased before June 18, 1987, the property must have been used principally in a farming business during at least five years that it was owned by the taxpayer or his or her ancestors.

If the farm was purchased after June 17, 1987, the taxpayer must have owned it for at least 24 months and their gross revenue from farming must have exceeded income from all other sources for at least that 24-month period. Farmers who acquired their farms before June 18, 1987, but made the election available in 1994 to report accrued capital gains on that farm property were deemed, in 1994, to have disposed of the farm property and to have reacquired it at the proceeds of disposition designated in that election. This "deemed reacquisition" means they must now follow the rules applicable to farms acquired after June 17, 1987.

The farmer is permitted to claim a reserve on that portion of the farm sale that is not yet payable, according to certain restrictions. If the farm is sold and a mortgage taken back from the purchaser, the vendor must report capital gains on the greater of: 20 per cent of the gain each year, or the amount of proceeds received. This can spread the tax from that capital over a period of up to five years. For a non-arm's-length sale, from a parent to a son for example, the minimum amount changes from 20 per cent to 10 per cent of the gain, and enables the vendor to effectively spread the tax over a period of up to 10 years.

Alternative minimum tax (AMT) — see description on page 165 — does not apply to the capital gain on the sale of eligible capital property (quota, for example). Nor does the AMT apply to any deemed dispositions in the year of death.

There are special, complicated rules for transferring farmland, eligible capital property and depreciable property of a prescribed class to a spouse/common-law partner or child during a taxpayer's lifetime or upon death. Interested readers should refer to the CRA's interpretation bulletins, IT268R4 — *Inter Vivos Transfer of Farm Property to a Child* and IT349R — *Intergenerational Transfer of Farm Property on Death.*

Currently, for example, all transfers of farmland situated in Ontario into a family-farm corporation are exempt from the Ontario land transfer tax (LTT). The Ontario government has expanded this provision to include qualified transfers of farmland between family members, as well as transfers from family farm corporations to individual family members for transactions that take place after March 25, 2008.

Given the complexities involved, it might therefore be prudent to consult with a Certified General Accountant and/or lawyer on matters related to the transfer or sale of farmland.

## Tax Tips

A child beneficiary of a trust who has never farmed could still possess qualified farm property, provided a relative — i.e., parent, grandparent or great-grandparent — satisfied the gross revenue test in previous generations when they owned and operated the farm on a regular, continuous basis.

## Other Measures

### Canadian Agricultural Income Stabilization (CAIS)

The Canadian Agricultural Income Stabilization (CAIS) Program is designed to provide Canadian agricultural producers with a long-term whole-farm risk management tool that provides protection for farming operations from both large and small declines in farm income.

For details about the CAIS program, consult the CAIS Handbook; call CAIS at 1-877-838-5144; contact your provincial ministry of agriculture; or consult with a Certified General Accountant familiar with this program.

## Crop Advances

Farmers are eligible for up to $100,000 in interest-free cash advances for stored crops under the *Agricultural Marketing Programs Act*. Advances of up to $400,000 are also available at market interest rates. The crop must be in storage in a non-processed form, while the producer must retain title to the crop and also be responsible for marketing it. This advance is considered a loan and it is not taxable when received. Income is triggered when the crop is sold and the loan repaid.

## Canadian Farm Business Advisory Services (CFBAS)

A financial management counselling program, entitled the Canadian Farm Business Advisory Services (CFBAS), is available for Canadian farmers who are experiencing agriculture-related financial problems. For a fee of $100, farmers can receive confidential counselling services to deal with problems such as decreased margins or cash flow difficulties.

Other specialized business planning services, at variable costs, are also available through the CFBAS.

Farmers in drought-stricken regions of Canada — which have been particularly prevalent in some venues in recent years — may also qualify for income tax relief. Consult Agriculture and Agri-Food Canada for details regarding current designated drought regions for specifically defined agricultural activities.

# INVESTMENT INCOME AND EXPENSES

## Interest: Annual Accrual

The interest income on compound-interest obligations, such as Canada Savings Bonds (CSB) or other instruments like guaranteed investment certificates (GIC) acquired after 1989, must be reported on an annual accrual basis from the anniversary date. Investment issuers are obligated to provide taxpayers with annual information slips (T5s) reporting this income, although it is the taxpayer's responsibility to ensure all interest is recorded.

## Dividends

Taxpayers who receive eligible dividends from a public Canadian corporation (and certain private, resident corporations that must pay Canadian tax at the general corporate rate) are subject to an enhanced dividend tax credit rate that includes a 45 per cent gross-up (up from the previous 25 per cent), offset by a federal dividend tax credit, which reduces federal income tax payable, worth roughly 19 per cent (18.97

per cent) of the total grossed-up amount (the actual reduction is 11/18ths of the 45 per cent gross-up). This equates to a dividend tax credit worth 27.5 per cent of actual dividends.

This enhanced dividend tax credit rate covers eligible dividends paid since January 1, 2006. Both public and private corporations whose dividends are subject to the enhanced rate must notify their shareholders of this status.

Ineligible dividends from Canadian-controlled private corporations (CCPC) not subject to the general corporate tax rate will continue to be subject to the 25 per cent gross-up, and 16.67 per cent dividend tax credit (or 13.33 per cent reduction to the total grossed-up amount).

The provinces and territories now have a two-tier dividend structure in place similar to that of the federal government. The following dividend tax credits are available in 2008 on eligible dividends received from public Canadian corporations and other private, resident corporations that pay Canadian tax at the general corporate rate:

| | |
|---|---|
| Alberta: | 9.00 per cent of eligible taxable dividends |
| British Columbia: | 12.00 per cent of eligible taxable dividends |
| Manitoba: | 11.00 per cent of eligible taxable dividends |
| New Brunswick: | 12.00 per cent of eligible taxable dividends |
| Newfoundland and Labrador: | 6.65 per cent of eligible taxable dividends |
| Northwest Territories: | 11.50 per cent of eligible taxable dividends |
| Nova Scotia: | 8.85 per cent of eligible taxable dividends |
| Nunavut: | 6.20 per cent of eligible taxable dividends |
| Ontario: | 7.00 per cent of eligible taxable dividends |
| Prince Edward Island: | 10.50 per cent of eligible taxable dividends |
| Quebec: | 11.90 per cent of eligible taxable dividends |
| Saskatchewan: | 11.00 per cent of eligible taxable dividends |
| Yukon: | 11.00 per cent of eligible taxable dividends |

The dividends from other corporations, based on the grossed-up amount, are taxed as follows:

| | |
|---|---|
| Alberta: | 4.50 per cent of taxable dividends |
| British Columbia: | 5.10 per cent of taxable dividends |
| Manitoba: | 3.15 per cent of taxable dividends |

| New Brunswick: | 5.30 per cent of taxable dividends |
| Newfoundland and Labrador: | 5.00 per cent of taxable dividends |
| Northwest Territories: | 6.00 per cent of taxable dividends |
| Nova Scotia: | 7.70 per cent of taxable dividends |
| Nunavut: | 4.00 per cent of taxable dividends |
| Ontario: | 5.13 per cent of taxable dividends |
| Prince Edward Island: | 4.30 per cent of taxable dividends |
| Quebec: | 8.00 per cent of taxable dividends |
| Saskatchewan: | 6.00 per cent of taxable dividends |
| Yukon: | 4.45 per cent of taxable dividends |

Check with your Certified General Accountant to determine the current status of dividend tax credits in your jurisdiction.

Although dividends from non-resident corporations must also be included in income, they are not subject to either the gross-up or dividend tax credit. Where foreign currency is involved, such dividends must be converted to Canadian dollars at the average rate of exchange for the year.

Stock dividends are generally treated as ordinary taxable dividends. This dividend amount also represents the cost of the new shares. If the stock dividend is in shares of the same class, it may affect the shareholder's average cost for future sales.

Common shareholders of a public corporation are sometimes entitled to apply their dividend proceeds toward the purchase of additional corporate shares at a discount from market price under a dividend reinvestment plan (DRIP). This will, in turn, incrementally increase the cost base of their investment.

Although such shareholders will, under a strict interpretation of the *Income Tax Act*, incur a taxable benefit equal to the discount amount when such shares are purchased, in practice the CRA does not assess a benefit where the amount paid for the additional shares is at least 95 per cent of their FMV and all shareholders are accorded the same reinvestment rights. Taxpayers are, however, still liable for tax otherwise payable on their dividends in the year such dividends have been reinvested.

Stock splits are not taxable.

## Capital Gains and Losses

A capital gain results from a sale or deemed disposition of a capital property, such as an investment-related instrument (i.e., stock), when it is sold for more than its ACB, less any disposition expenses incurred, like commissions. Unlike ordinary income however, only 50 per cent of the gain is included in income.

When the investor experiences a loss, the 50 per cent "allowable capital loss" amount must first be used to offset any capital gains they may have in the same year. Any unused allowable capital loss amount may be carried back up to three years or forward indefinitely to reduce taxable capital gains of other years.

The inclusion rate for capital gains and losses has not always been 50 per cent. In 2000, for instance, the inclusion rate was decreased twice — from 75 per cent to 66.67 per cent, then to 50 per cent. Individuals may therefore need to make complex adjustments when applying capital losses of one year against capital gains of another.

The proceeds of disposition from capital property have sometimes been ruled by the courts to be ordinary income or losses rather than capital gains or losses if there is strong evidence that the nature of such a transaction was purely speculative — i.e., the property was purchased with the short-term intent to sell. Other factors, such as the number of transactions; duration of holdings; amount of time devoted to carrying them out; means of financing; and expertise of the taxpayer, may also weigh into the decision. The CRA also addresses some of these factors in its bulletin IT459 — *Adventure or Concern in the Nature of Trade*.

Special rules exist for capital gains and losses originating from certain foreign currency transactions where there is a fluctuation in foreign exchange rates. Your Certified General Accountant can help determine whether these rules are applicable to you.

## Capital Gains Deduction

Capital gains from dispositions of qualified farm and fishing property, as well as small business corporation (SBC) shares, may be eligible for a taxpayer's lifetime exemption of up to $750,000 effective on or after

March 19, 2007 (increased from $500,000 prior to that date). At a 50 per cent inclusion rate, this represents a taxable amount of $375,000 (up from $250,000).

An individual's ability to claim the capital gains deduction may be reduced by past claims for capital gains deductions, allowable business investment losses (ABIL) (see page 75) or a cumulative net investment loss (CNIL) (see page 76).

## Reserves

If a property sale results in a capital gain, and a portion of the proceeds are not due until after the year end, taxpayers may claim a reasonable reserve for the unrealized portion of that gain. At least one-fifth of the capital gain must be included in income each year unless it arises from the sale of a farm, qualified fishing business or shares in an SBC to the taxpayer's child. In that case at least one-tenth of the gain must be included in income annually.

A reserve for the unrealized portion of an ordinary income gain may be claimed for up to 36 months from the date of the sale (unless the proceeds become due earlier) if:

- the sale of land results in an ordinary income gain and a portion of the proceeds are not due until after the taxation year end; or
- the sale of property other than land results in an ordinary income gain and a portion of that gain is due more than two years after the sale date.

A reserve claimed in one year must be taken into income the next year and a new reserve, if still applicable, claimed at the end of that year.

## Shares of a Small Business Corporation (SBC)

A small business corporation (SBC) is a CCPC in which all or substantially all of its assets (generally representing at least 90 per cent of FMV) at the time of sale were:

- used in an active business carried on primarily in Canada (more than 50 per cent) by a corporation or any related corporation(s); or
- shares or debt of one or more connected corporation(s) which also qualify as an SBC.

A connected shareholder is defined by the *Income Tax Act* as one who owns at least 10 per cent of the issued shares of any class of stock in a corporation (or related corporation). The CRA also takes into account the right of an individual to acquire additional shares when making this calculation.

To qualify for the $750,000 capital gains deduction, shares of an SBC (including connected corporations, which are considered to be associated and therefore part of the same unit) must meet several requirements. Throughout the 24 months immediately prior to disposition, for instance, the shares must have been owned either by the taxpayer or a related person or partnership. Throughout that same period, more than 50 per cent of the FMV of a corporation's assets must have been used in an active business carried on in Canada and/or be shares or debt of a qualified connected corporation.

The requirement to hold shares for 24 months does not apply to treasury shares issued as consideration for other shares or the assets used in an active business. A special provision also applies for qualified SBC shares when the company goes public. Taxpayers may elect to dispose of their small business shares immediately prior to the corporation going public. Where the shares' FMV exceeds their ACB, investors may specify any amount between those values as proceeds of disposition and then recognize a capital gain, to be offset by the available capital gains deduction.

Individuals may defer the tax on capital gains from eligible small business investments, provided such proceeds are reinvested in another eligible small business. Eligible small business investments include newly issued shares in an SBC whose assets do not exceed $50 million. An eligible reinvestment can be made at any time during the year of disposition or within 120 days after the end of the year.

In practice, the classification of an SBC and applications involving its subsidiaries can sometimes be complex. Consult your Certified General Accountant for guidance in this area.

## Tax Tips

Consider transferring non-active assets to a separate company to maintain qualified SBC status.

If you transfer a qualified SBC share into a self-directed RRSP, the amount of time such shares are held inside the RRSP counts towards the 24-month holding period restriction.

## Allowable Business Investment Loss (ABIL)

A loss realized from the arm's-length sale of shares or qualifying debt of an SBC may qualify as a business investment loss. Similarly, a loss upon the deemed disposition of an uncollectible debt of an SBC or the shares of a bankrupt SBC may qualify. Taxpayers might also be able to claim, via an election on their tax return, an allowable business investment loss (ABIL) if they continue to hold shares or debt in an SBC that has become insolvent.

A business investment loss is calculated the same way as a capital loss, except that it may be applied against all income, not just capital gains. One-half of the business investment loss may be applied against other income in the year the loss is realized. Unused portions of an allowable business investment loss may be carried back 3 years, with the balance carried forward 10 years. If any unapplied ABIL balance remains at the end of 10 years attributable to losses sustained after 2003 (or at the end of 7 years for losses attributable prior to 2004), it then becomes a net capital loss, which can be used to reduce taxable capital gains thereafter.

The deductible amount of an individual's ABIL must first be reduced by any previously claimed capital gains deduction. If any allowable business investment loss is deducted from income, an equal amount of taxable capital gains must be realized and reported as income in subsequent years before the capital gains deduction becomes available.

Where a corporation is insolvent and neither it nor a corporation controlled by it carries on business, the taxpayer will be allowed to elect a disposition for tax purposes and realize the loss. If that corporation, or another controlled by it, commences carrying on business within 24 months, the taxpayer must recognize a gain equal to the loss claimed in the year the business recommences.

An election must be made under the *Income Tax Act* to claim a loss on debt, or shares of an insolvent company. This requirement also applies to claiming capital losses even where the company is (was) public.

## Tax Tips

Keep all documentation related to an ABIL. It may be required as proof to substantiate your claim.

## Cumulative Net Investment Loss (CNIL)

A taxpayer's cumulative net investment loss (CNIL) at the end of a year is defined as the amount by which the total of investment expenses incurred after 1987 exceeds the total of their investment income for those years.

The cumulative gains limit for purposes of the capital gains deduction will be reduced by the amount of an individual's CNIL balance at the end of a taxation year.

## Income Trusts

Income trusts are investment instruments that distribute cash from revenue generating assets directly to unit holders in a tax-efficient manner — often without having to pay any tax at the corporate level. As such, they have proven to be a popular vehicle for both many businesses and individual investors, since assets held in a trust structure tend to be more highly valued in comparison to other corporate structures.

The activity of such trusts, now also formally known as specified investment flow-through (SIFT) trusts, has been sharply curtailed, however, after Canada's Finance Minister announced significant changes to the income trust taxation structure in October 2006. These have resulted in the distributions from such trusts being taxed more like dividends from corporations.

The structural changes announced took effect in 2007 for certain trusts, such as new trusts, that were not publicly traded until after October 2006; they will not apply until the 2011 taxation year for other trusts that were publicly traded prior to November 2006 and whose growth in the intervening period does not exceed what the Department of Finance defines as "normal growth." Certain real estate investment trusts (REIT) meeting specified criteria are exempt from the new rules.

Income trust structures that are still allowed under the new rules might appeal to investors who are interested in a steady cash flow return. Such investors should note, however, that a component of the cash flow from income trust investments might constitute a return of capital, as opposed to income. This return of capital results in a lower cost base, thus leading to a larger capital gain when such investments are disposed of.

Due to the complexity of income trust taxation and the new restrictions placed upon such structures, it is best to check with your Certified General Accountant if income trusts are part of your investment strategy.

## Interest Expense Deductibility

Interest expenses on borrowed funds between arm's-length parties who are engaging in transactions at commercial interest rates are deductible provided the taxpayer uses the funds to produce income from a business, investment or property. The same provisions might also apply as a result of a loan between non-arm's-length parties provided FMV is received and the recipient pays interest on the loan.

Interest expense on funds borrowed to make an interest-free loan might also be eligible for deduction in certain instances where it can be proven that such funds are ultimately used to earn, or enhance income-earning capability.

A taxpayer can also deduct fees (but not commissions) paid for advice received with respect to the purchase, sale and administration of specific investments, such as shares or securities, provided those fees are paid to a professional whose principal business involves managing such investments.

Decisions handed down by the Supreme Court of Canada (Singleton, Ludco Enterprises Ltd.) in September 2001 reinforced the right of taxpayers to deduct interest where borrowed money was used for the purpose of earning income from a business or property. Lower courts had earlier denied the taxpayers their respective deductions.

The Supreme Court ruled that in the absence of evidence of a sham, window-dressing or other similar circumstances, the courts could neither question whether other "economic realities" served as motivation behind a subsequent transaction (Singleton), nor could they question the sufficiency of the income expected or received (Ludco).

However, this remains a very sensitive area of tax law, and lower court rulings since then have not necessarily been consistent with those results (i.e., Lipson). Therefore, it is best that you consult your Certified General Accountant for advice about appropriate tax strategies involving complex transactions.

## Superficial Losses

The *Income Tax Act* contains specific rules with respect to the treatment of superficial losses. The superficial loss provision — which begins 30 days before and ends 30 days after the disposition of a property — exists to prevent a taxpayer from executing a transaction that creates a loss while they, or an affiliated person or corporation, retain or acquire control of the same, or an identical property as that which created the loss.

Consult your Certified General Accountant for details about which types of dispositions would constitute superficial losses.

## Principal Residences

The gain realized by an individual on a principal residence disposition is not included in income and is therefore tax exempt.

A principal residence includes the immediately adjacent land, generally considered to be up to one-half hectare (about 1.24 acres), unless any excess land can objectively be demonstrated to have contributed to the use and enjoyment of the housing unit as a residence. As the determination of any additional exempt portion for the purpose of this gain is complex, you are advised to contact your Certified General Accountant to assist with this calculation.

Before 1982, individuals were able to arrange their affairs such that if they owned two properties (e.g., a residence and a cottage), the residence could be registered in the name of one spouse and the cottage in the other's name. This resulted in the husband and wife both enjoying the benefit of owning two principal residences, while avoiding taxation on the disposition of either property.

For 1982 and subsequent years, a family unit has only been permitted one principal residence for purposes of this exemption. A couple that owned two principle residences prior to 1982, and who still own both, could possibly enjoy the benefit of two principal residence exemptions on gains that had accrued up until December 31, 1981.

It is also still possible to obtain the benefits of two principal residence exemptions by transferring one of the properties (preferably one that has not appreciated substantially in value) to a son or daughter over the age of 17 who currently does not own a principal residence. When that property is subsequently disposed of, the adult child may claim the principal residence exemption and avoid taxation on disposition, provided it qualifies as their residence. A complex calculation to determine which property generates the higher exempt capital gain may be required. Your Certified General Accountant can help with this.

Because a principal residence is considered personal-use property, a taxpayer cannot realize a capital loss if, when they sold their home, its value had depreciated from the time it was purchased.

In some instances, certain individuals who are involved in the business of selling homes may be denied the principal residence exemption if the CRA deems that resale was a motive in the acquisition of a particular property. A dispute could arise with the CRA regarding whether a house sold constitutes a principal residence or is part of a business transaction, based on factors such as the length of ownership; type of property being sold; frequency of home purchase/sale; and the taxpayer's original intent when purchasing the property.

Couples who are involved in divorce proceedings might enter into a settlement that involves transferring ownership in a house and/or cottage. This could, in turn, involve issues such as the timing of the principal residence designation — especially for a cottage — and the adjusted cost base at which the transfer takes place.

Consult your Certified General Accountant, especially in situations where complex questions arise about the principal residence designation.

## Tax Tips

When selling your principal residence, you would be prudent to fill out CRA Form T2091 — *Designation of a Property as a Principal Residence by an Individual,* especially in situations where doubt could arise with respect to any part of the amount you are claiming.

A principal residence can include a house, apartment, condominium, duplex unit, cottage, mobile home trailer or houseboat.

# Personal-Use Property

There are two main categories of personal-use property. One is also termed "personal use-property." The other is "listed personal property" (LPP). While both categories refer to property that is held primarily for personal enjoyment, and not commercial use, items characterized as LPP are specific and include:

- a print, etching, drawing, painting, sculpture or other similar work of art;
- jewellery;
- rare folio, rare manuscript or rare book;
- stamp; or
- coin.

From a tax perspective, both types of personal-use property are considered to have both an adjusted cost base as well as proceeds upon disposition of at least $1,000; as a result, they cannot produce a capital gain unless disposed of for greater than $1,000. Most personal-use property losses are considered personal expenses, and are therefore not deductible. Only LPP can produce a capital loss, subject to strict rules. For example, capital losses arising from LPP can only be offset against capital gains specifically arising from LPP. If LPP losses cannot be offset by LPP gains in the same year, they can be applied against previous LPP gains not already offset up to three years back; or against future gains for up to seven years.

Consult your Certified General Accountant for details.

# PERSONAL DEDUCTIONS

## Child Care Expenses

A claim may be made for expenses incurred on behalf of an eligible child to allow an individual or their spouse or common-law partner to:

- earn income from employment or self-employment;
- spend at least 12 hours per month studying in an educational program lasting at least three consecutive weeks at a secondary school, college, university or other designated educational institution;
- take an occupational training course for which either spouse or common-law partner received an allowance under the *National Training Act*; or
- conduct research or similar work for which either spouse or common-law partner received a grant.

Generally, the parent with the lower net income claims the least of:

- the actual amount paid;
- two-thirds of that parent's earned income; or
- $10,000 for each child on whose behalf a disability tax credit may be claimed, regardless of age; plus $7,000 per each other eligible child under age 7 at year end; plus $4,000 for each other eligible child between the ages of 7 and 16, inclusive (extending past age 16 only for children that have a physical or mental infirmity and remain dependant on the taxpayer or their spouse).

For parents of children with a disability, there is no requirement that the parent claiming the child care expenses for eligible services such as baby-sitting, or those provided at a day nursery or day care centre, among others, be the one who claims the disability tax credit (DTC) on behalf of an eligible child. In many cases it will be advantageous for the other parent to claim the DTC. In some cases the child, after having attained the age of majority, might be able to claim the DTC.

Single parents may also claim a deduction for child care expenses incurred during the months they pursued full or part-time education at a designated institution. In two-parent families where one spouse or common-law partner is working while the other is studying full or part-time, the higher income spouse is eligible to claim a deduction.

These available deductions, calculated by formula, closely parallel the claim criteria listed above. Check with your Certified General Accountant to determine which options are applicable to you.

Note also that:

Payments made to a boarding school or camp, including a sports school that requires lodging qualify up to a maximum of $175 per week per child under 7 and a maximum of $100 per week for other eligible children between 7 and 16, inclusive.

A maximum of $250 per week can be claimed for all children under the age of 17 for whom anyone is entitled to claim a DTC.

Under certain conditions, the supporting person with the higher income will be able to claim child care expenses, with the same limitation of $175 per week for each child under 7 or that has a severe disability, plus $100 per week for other eligible children. An example would be where the parents pursue full- or part-time education, as described earlier in this section (although for part-time education the corresponding amounts eligible for deduction are $175/$100 per month, respectively).

Parents who have shared custody of a child over the course of a taxation year might each be entitled to claim a deduction for eligible expenses incurred while that child resided with them.

Child care expenses claimed might reduce the amount eligible for the taxpayer to claim as a child tax benefit.

Eligible children include the taxpayer's or their spouse's or common-law partner's natural or adopted children, or one in respect of whom the individual had custody and contributed to his/her support; who were under 16 at any time in the year; or dependent by reason of mental or physical infirmity.

The cost of summer day camps, sports schools or other recreational activities may also qualify as deductible child care expenses depending on factors such as the child's age, the program's sophistication (i.e., if it is oriented more towards achieving a progressive, measurable improvement in skills, rather than serving as a recreational sporting activity, the CRA would generally not equate that to child care), and whether such expenses are incurred to allow the parent or supporting person to carry on earning a living. Court cases have also emphasized that the expenses incurred should relate primarily to guardianship, protection and child care.

## Tax Tips

Although supporting parties must be earning a living in order to deduct child care expenses, this deduction might still be available during periods in which temporary, extenuating circumstances, such as a strike or other labour stoppage prevent you from working. Furthermore, there may be other instances when child care expenses remain deductible because the services provided help enable a parent to earn a living or attend classes, even though the services were not provided at the exact time they were at work or school.

The child care portion of fees paid to a private school that provides both educational and child care services (such as before or after-class supervision) might also be deductible as child care expenses.

There may be situations where grandparents are supporting their grandchildren and are therefore able to claim child care expenses as the primary caregiver.

## Spousal Support Payments

Spousal support payments, which used to be more commonly referred to as alimony and maintenance payments, are deductible by the payer and taxable to the recipient, defined as the "spouse or common-law partner or former spouse or common-law partner of the payer," provided certain conditions are met. Generally, the payer and recipient must be living apart as a result of the relationship breakdown, both when payments are received and for the balance of that year; also, payments must be an allowance made periodically, either directly or to a third party under a written agreement or court order.

A lump-sum payment stipulated in any legal arrangement would not constitute a periodic payment and therefore probably not qualify as being tax-deductible by the payer. However, where the legal agreement specifies that a periodic payment take place and the payer makes a lump-sum payment in respect of arrears under that agreement, then that payment would probably qualify as being tax deductible by the payer, with the recipient having to include it with his or her taxable income.

Payments made before a written agreement or court order has been issued are also deductible to the payer and taxable to the recipient if the agreement or order specifically provides that payments made earlier in the year or the immediately preceding year qualify.

Expenses specifically determined by a court order or written agreement as being payable directly to a third party for spousal support are also deductible and taxable to the respective parties.

## Child Support Payments

Child support payments are treated differently. Recipients do not include child support payments in their income, nor does the payer deduct such payments for tax purposes, if they originated pursuant to a written agreement or court order made on or after May 1, 1997, or before that date if the payment commencement date pursuant to the original agreement, or a varied version thereof, was on or after May 1, 1997.

Prior to that date, child support paid pursuant to a written agreement or court order was deductible by the payer and taxable to the recipient. Parents with existing agreements made before May 1, 1997, upon which payments had also commenced prior to that day, have the option of filing a joint election with the CRA to apply the new tax treatment to payments made after April 30, 1997. Once the tax treatment has been changed, however, parties will not be permitted to return to the old rules.

In order for an allowance to qualify as child support, it should generally be payable on a periodic basis (typically weekly or monthly), with provisions to continue for either an indefinite period or until the occurrence of a specified future event, such as a child attaining the age of majority.

## Issues Related to Spousal and Child Support

Legal fees incurred to establish spousal or child support are deductible. Should a portion of the legal fees paid in a divorce settlement be for obtaining child support, the onus is on the taxpayer to establish the proportion of fees directly related to child support.

Legal costs incurred to enforce pre-existing rights to interim or permanent support amounts, to increase spousal and/or child support, or to defend against (but not for) the reduction of support payments (whether child support or otherwise) are both deductible, provided they are not incurred against an estate.

The CRA used to rule that legal fees incurred in establishing the right to spousal support amounts were not deductible because such costs were for personal or living expenses. However, the Agency has changed its position and now considers legal costs incurred to obtain spousal support under the *Divorce Act* or applicable provincial legislation in a separation agreement, to have been incurred as a result of enforcing a pre-existing right to support and therefore deductible.

Similarly, the CRA has also changed its position with regard to legal costs incurred by a taxpayer to increase spousal or child support once an original court-imposed settlement has been passed. These are also now deductible.

Taxpayers must also be cognizant of any relevant provincial or territorial laws with respect to support or maintenance that might apply to them.

### Tax Tips

Be aware that if you go to court and obtain an amending order to an existing agreement, the income tax rules attributable to each may be different, particularly if the original agreement was made prior to May 1, 1997, and the amendment occurred on or after that date.

Legal agreements should specify the breakdown, if any, between support payments that are for spousal support and child support. Otherwise, it will be assumed for tax purposes they are all for child support and treated accordingly by the CRA.

You may claim eligible support payments made to a payee living outside Canada if you have adequate proof of payment; in most cases, the CRA will ask for a court order and/or written agreement and payment receipts to allow this deduction. Therefore, you should retain these documents in order to support your claim.

## Moving Expenses

Taxpayers may claim eligible moving expenses to change residences within Canada, provided the move brings them at least 40 kilometres closer (using the shortest normal route) to a new job, business location in Canada or post-secondary institution at which they begin full-time attendance.

The claim amount is limited to income from the new business or employment, or prizes and research grants, either in the year of the move or the following year. For individuals who are reimbursed in whole or in part, the full amount of the moving expense can only be claimed as a deduction if the reimbursement amount is also included in calculating income.

Students that were in full-time attendance at a post-secondary educational institution in Canada and who move at least 40 kilometres within Canada for employment purposes may also claim moving expenses against income earned from a full or part-time job (including a summer job) the year the move took place or the following year. This also applies the year after graduation.

Eligible moving expenses include such items as:

- travel costs, including reasonable amounts for meals and accommodation to move the individual and members of their household;
- storage costs for household effects;
- costs for up to 15 days of temporary board and lodging near either residence;
- the cost of cancelling a lease or selling the old residence as a result of the move;
- the cost of connecting or disconnecting utilities as a result of the move;
- legal fees;
- reasonable selling costs directly related to the sale of the home; and
- transfer taxes or taxes upon registration of title to the new residence only if a former residence has been sold.

Additional expenses with respect to maintaining a vacant former residence, such as mortgage interest, property taxes, insurance premiums, maintenance of heat, power and utility connections, along with certain personal costs to revise legal documents to reflect the new address, are also deductible. The deductible amounts are limited to the lesser of actual costs involved in maintaining the former premises, or $5,000.

A taxpayer who rents out a former home in their original location prior to moving because they are unable to sell it might be able to claim rental income and losses in connection with that property.

Limited tax-free compensation may be available where an employer reimburses an employee to cover for a loss or diminishment in the value of their former home. Compensation of up to $15,000 for an eligible housing loss is tax free. If the compensation exceeds $15,000, half that excess is taxable.

Under certain circumstances, a taxpayer that is required to move into a temporary home before moving a second time into a permanent home might be able to deduct expenses related to both moves. In determining whether a home is considered temporary or permanent in nature, the tax courts are likely to look at a variety of factors such as whether or not certain of the taxpayer's material belongings remain in storage and whether or not family members have relocated with the taxpayer.

Furthermore, taxpayers who move to a new location and work there for only a short period of time (i.e., a few months), before moving a second time for employment reasons — perhaps back to their original venue — might be able to claim expenses for two moves provided they can prove they were "ordinarily resident" in terms of being settled into the daily routine of life, while in both places.

Moving expenses might also be deductible in certain circumstances that involve a move in or out of Canada, provided the taxpayer is and remains a Canadian resident.

## Tax Tips

You do not necessarily need to have a job already lined up at your new location in order to become eligible to deduct moving expenses against earned income when you eventually find and begin work at the new venue within a reasonable period of time. An example of this could involve a situation where a taxpayer moves from one geographic location to another in Canada where employment opportunities are better.

If a former home is sold for a loss in a year subsequent to relocation, taxpayers might have the opportunity to select in which of those two years it is most beneficial to claim that loss for tax purposes. Consult your Certified General Accountant if this situation applies to you.

## Travel Expense Claims

Taxpayers have the option of using a simplified method to calculate certain non-reimbursed travel expenses specifically related to a move, medical treatment, or for northern resident deductions. Such travel can, for example, occur by automobile, bus, train or airplane and cover such items as hotel or motel accommodations, meals and other incidental expenses. This simplified method includes a flat rate of $17 per meal (to a maximum of $51 per day) per person.

Special rates apply to transportation sector employees, who can use the rate of $17 per meal (up to a maximum of $51 per day). In addition, transportation sector employees, such as those involved in the trucking, railroad, bus or airline industries to transport people and/or goods, can use the Canadian equivalent of US$17 per meal (up to a maximum of US$51 per day) while travelling and incurring meal expenses in the United States.

Receipts do not have to be submitted when claiming these flat rates, although taxpayers should keep their receipts in case they are asked by the CRA to support their claim. Employees who elect to claim actual meal expenses must keep their receipts in order to claim.

The *Income Tax Act* allows employees to deduct 50 per cent of meal expenses, regardless of whether they elect to do so via fixed or actual rates.

The simplified method also includes a fixed amount to be claimed per kilometre of travel in each province or territory (where interprovincial/territorial travel is involved, the venue from which the journey began is used for calculation purposes). The applicable rates for the provinces and territories in 2007 were as follows:

| | |
|---|---|
| Alberta: | 48.0 cents per kilometre |
| British Columbia: | 48.0 cents per kilometre |
| Manitoba: | 46.5 cents per kilometre |
| New Brunswick: | 47.0 cents per kilometre |
| Newfoundland and Labrador: | 50.5 cents per kilometre |
| Northwest Territories: | 56.5 cents per kilometre |
| Nova Scotia: | 48.0 cents per kilometre |
| Nunavut: | 56.5 cents per kilometre |
| Ontario: | 49.5 cents per kilometre |
| Prince Edward Island: | 47.0 cents per kilometre |
| Quebec: | 52.5 cents per kilometre |
| Saskatchewan: | 46.0 cents per kilometre |
| Yukon: | 58.0 cents per kilometre |

Changes for the following year are typically published by the federal government either late in the old calendar year or early in the new one; therefore, possible updated rates for the 2008 taxation year were not yet available when this book went to press.

> ### Tax Tips
>
> Foot and bicycle couriers, along with rickshaw drivers, qualify for a meal reduction of $17 daily, without receipts.

## Northern Residents Deductions

Special deductions relating to residency and travel are available to taxpayers who reside in designated northern areas defined as either a "prescribed northern zone" or a "prescribed intermediate zone" (which collectively encompass all three territories, plus parts of Canadian provinces with the exception of those in the Maritime region) for a continuous period of not less than six months beginning or ending in the year. Such venues are listed in CRA Form T4039.

Taxpayers in a prescribed northern zone are, as a result of increases in the 2008 federal budget, eligible for a basic residency deduction of up to $8.25 per day, or $16.50 if they are claiming on behalf of the entire household, even if there is only one member in that household (those amounts are up from $7.50 and $15.00, respectively).

Taxpayers in a prescribed intermediate zone are eligible for one-half the amount of the northern deduction — $4.13 for individual taxpayers, and $8.25 per household (up from $3.75 and $7.50, respectively).

In some instances, these deductions might help offset the inclusion in income of a cost of living differential, or premium, paid to certain taxpayers who reside in places such as Canada's three territories. Such premiums are designed to compensate for living in more isolated areas that have a higher cost of living and require greater travel expenses.

Supplementary housing benefits are also available for residents in prescribed zones that do not have a developed rental market.

Taxpayers claiming Northern Residents Deductions must fill in CRA Form T2222 and attach it to their income tax return.

# PART TWO: TAX PLANNING ISSUES

## INCOME SPLITTING

Income splitting with a spouse or other family member in situations where this is legally permitted can be an effective way of saving the family unit tax — sometimes a very substantial amount. However, there are stringent rules in place designed to prevent income splitting in certain

### Tax Tips

If you earn more than your spouse, you could reduce your family's combined tax bill by paying your spouse's expenses, thus allowing them to save their money for investment purposes. The income and gains from these investments would then be taxed in your spouse's hands at their (presumably lower) tax rate. This strategy will also help you even out future retirement income if you have been able to invest in a tax-deferred retirement plan and your spouse has not.

instances, so it is necessary to know where these opportunities exist and where they do not in order to carry out proper tax planning.

## Attribution Rules

The *Income Tax Act* includes rules that cause income to be attributed to and taxed in another person's hands in specific instances. For example, income earned from money or other property loaned to a spouse/common-law partner, related minor or trusts of which they are beneficiaries, is attributed back to lenders except in defined circumstances as discussed below.

Loans made to any related adult will result in income attribution if one of the main reasons for the loan is to reduce or avoid tax on income from loaned or substituted property. Such rules also apply to situations where a low-interest or no-interest note is taken back when one family member transfers property to another.

### Tax Tips

If you earn less than your spouse, keep a clear record of the source of your investment funds to ensure that your investment income is attributed to you. This could be accomplished by, for instance, depositing your personal income into a separate bank account rather than a joint account. Then those funds could be used to make investments in your name.

Income earned from Canada Child Tax Benefit (CCTB) payments invested in the child's name will not be attributed back to the parents (see Additional Tax Considerations on page 162).

To further discourage income splitting with minor children, a special tax at top marginal rates applies to certain income received by minor children under the age of 18. Generally, this special tax applies to the receipt of dividends and other shareholder benefits from private corporation shares, as well as income received from a partnership or trust that provides property or services to a business in which a relative of that child participates.

## Attribution of Capital Gains

Attribution generally applies to any capital gain realized by a spouse or common-law partner on property loaned or transferred at less than FMV. Therefore, when there is a gain on the disposition of such a property, reinvestment of the full proceeds constitutes a substituted property, and all gains from the new property would also be attributed back to the owner of the original property.

However, a capital gain realized by a child or other related minor is not subject to attribution, except for certain farm property transferred under a tax-deferred rollover. Attribution will not apply where capital gains have been earned in an irrevocable trust established for a child (minor or otherwise).

Parents often contribute to investment accounts held in trust for their children. To avoid attribution of capital gains in that instance, care should be taken that such "in trust for" accounts qualify as irrevocable trusts. To qualify, the terms and conditions of the account must serve to divest, deprive or dispossess the parents of title to deposited funds. If the parent has the right to withdraw those funds for their personal benefit, the account will not qualify as an irrevocable trust.

## Tax Tips

Be careful how trust property is used to benefit minors. In one decision handed down by the Tax Court of Canada, three child beneficiaries were found to be joint and severally liable for a trust's taxes owing after a parent used some of the trust's proceeds to pay for their private school tuition and summer camp fees.

## Transfers for Fair Value

Transferred property for which fair market value (FMV) consideration is received is not subject to attribution rules. Taxpayers who transfer property to a spouse or common-law partner must elect that spousal rollover rules do not apply in order to avoid being subject to attribution rules. Through this election, the transferor may report any accrued gain up to that time. Their spouse will then report any future gain realized.

Where property is sold to a related person for less than its FMV, the seller is deemed to have received consideration equal to its FMV. Moreover, the family unit might ultimately end up paying double tax on a portion of any accrued capital gains. That is because the recipient will be taxed on any gains made on top of the original purchase price, part of which — the amount necessary to hike the selling price back up to FMV — will have already been reported by the seller.

## Tax Tips

Be aware that if you have any tax liabilities outstanding at the time you transfer property in a non-arm's-length transaction — i.e., to a spouse or other family member — especially where you have received less than fair market value consideration in return, they might, under some circumstances, be deemed by the tax courts as being joint and severally liable and therefore partially responsible for your liability.

## Loans for Fair Value

If a loan is made, or transferred property is settled with a loan, attribution rules do not apply provided:

- interest is charged on the loan at the lesser of a normal commercial rate or CRA's prescribed rate; and
- interest in respect of that year and each preceding year has been paid no later than 30 days after the end of each year.

If taxpayers loan funds to their spouse or common-law partner, with interest payable at least annually at the lesser of prescribed or commercial rates, and the spouse/common-law partner invests those funds to achieve a yield exceeding the rate of interest charged, that excess income will be taxed in the spouse or common-law partner's hands, not attributed back to the taxpayer.

## Loans to Earn Business Income

The *Income Tax Act* clearly distinguishes between business and property income. Attribution rules do not apply to income earned from a business — either as a proprietorship, partnership or through an SBC. Attribution will apply, however, if the borrower is a limited partner, or a partner who is not actively engaged in the activities of the partnership or a similar business.

Loans to family members, if used in an active business, will not result in attribution of the proceeds of any subsequent business income or gains.

## Reinvestment of Attributed Income

While earned income may be attributed back to the lender, the reinvestment of that income is for the recipient's account and will not be subject to attribution.

### Tax Tips

A loan may be preferable to an outright transfer, since after realizing the gain the transferee could repay the loan and invest the gain, free of future attribution. If cash is not readily available, consider lending investments. Note, however, that these rules can be complex; for instance, if the entire proceeds from the sale of the investment are reinvested, attribution will still apply. Seek advice from your Certified General Accountant.

## Statutory Income Splitting

CPP benefits of up to 50 per cent of an individual's total benefit may be assigned for spousal payment provided both spouses/common-law partners are at least 60 years of age. The percentage eligible for assignment is subject to certain considerations.

One spouse/common-law partner's assignment will automatically result in an assignment, in the same proportion, of the other spouse/common-law partner's direct benefit. Attribution rules do not apply to CPP benefits assigned in this manner.

## Tax Tips

If you and your spouse or common-law partner are receiving approximately the same level of benefit prior to an assignment, splitting CPP benefits will not likely be worthwhile. But if one partner receives greater benefits and has a higher taxable income than the other — particularly if this places them in a higher marginal tax bracket — you may achieve some advantage.

## Pension Income Splitting

Taxpayers are allowed to split pension income with their spouse or common-law partner, by allocating up to one-half of their qualified income, beginning in 2007. See also Pension Income Credit on page 148.

## Spousal Registered Retirement Savings Plans

For details on how the Spousal Registered Retirement Savings Plan (RRSP) can be used for long-term tax planning purposes, including future income splitting, see Spousal Registered Retirement Savings Plans on page 108.

## Registered Education Savings Plans (RESP)

Registered education savings plans (RESP) are established for a child, usually by a parent and/or grandparent, to help save for their post-secondary education. Contributions are made with after-tax dollars, and are not deductible for tax purposes.

The 2008 federal budget announced that contributions to an RESP will be allowed for a maximum of 31 years after the plan is established; 35 years if the beneficiary is disabled and eligible to claim the disability tax credit (DTC), up from 21 years and 25 years, respectively. The income earned within an RESP may be sheltered from tax for a maximum of 35 years-up to 40 years if the beneficiary is eligible to claim the DTC and he or she is the sole beneficiary of the plan (up from 25 years, and 30 years, respectively.) It is not taxable until used to finance post-secondary education costs, at which time it will be included in the recipient's income, presumably at a lower rate than that of the contributor. The original contributions are not taxable when withdrawn.

As a result of changes announced in the 2007 federal budget, there is no annual contribution limit for an RESP. However, total lifetime contributions are restricted to a maximum of $50,000 per beneficiary.

Prior to 2007, payments to beneficiaries of educational assistance payments (EAP) could only be made to full-time students enrolled in qualifying post-secondary educational programs, or to part-time students who could not be enrolled as full-time students because of physical or mental impairment. Effective in 2007, however, part-time students who are not physically or mentally impaired and who are enrolled in specified educational programs may be eligible to receive EAPs.

EAPs represent distributions of accumulated income and Canada Education Savings Grants (CESG). All contributions made to the RESP by the subscriber can be returned to that subscriber when the contract ends or at any time before, subject to the terms and conditions of the RESP. The returned contributions will not be taxable.

Taxpayers may change the named beneficiaries or designate more than one subject to the plan issuer's restrictions (although beneficiaries must be named before the age of 31, up from 21 previously).

Should taxpayers designate more than one beneficiary, each must be related to them. Under these so-called "family plans," one sibling's share may be paid to another sibling without attracting penalties. In other words, taxpayers are able to maximize contributions for two children, but one child can receive all the accumulated income if the other does not attend a post-secondary institution.

Contributions under a family RESP cannot be made for beneficiaries after they turn 31, (up from 21 beginning in 2008); if the single beneficiary has a disability, that period can be extended to age 35 (up from 25).

RESP income can be transferred to the contributor if the RESP is at least 10 years old and none of the intended beneficiaries attend post-secondary institutions by age 31 — up from 21 (although both the 10-year and age-31 conditions are waived if the beneficiary is mentally impaired).

Under those conditions, up to $50,000 in RESP income may be transferred to a subscriber's RRSP or spousal RRSP provided he or she has the contribution room. Otherwise, RESP-accumulated proceeds will be included in the subscriber's income and a 20 per cent tax will apply, in addition to regular taxes.

## Canada Education Savings Grant (CESG)

For every dollar a parent, grandparent or other person contributes toward the RESP of a child up to the age of 18, the federal government will contribute an additional 20 cents up to an annual limit of $500 for a $2,500 contribution (up from $400 for a $2,000 contribution in 2006 and prior years) through the Canada Education Savings Grant (CESG). Special rules apply to contributions made on behalf of 16- and 17-year-olds.

Families with net family income of up to $37,885 in 2008 are entitled to a higher CESG grant each year of 40 cents for every dollar on their first $500 of RESP contributions. Families with net family income between $37,885 and $75,769 are eligible for a higher grant of 30 cents per dollar each year on their first $500 of contributions.

For 2008, the maximum annual amount of CESG (basic + additional) that can be paid in any year is $600 for current contributions, and $1,100 if there is unused grant room from previous years. Unused grant room accumulates at a rate of $500 a year (up from $400 in 2006 and prior years).

The maximum lifetime CESG that a child is eligible for remains $7,200.

## Registered Disability Savings Plan (RDSP)

The 2007 federal budget introduced a new registered disability savings plan (RDSP), which is designed to provide savings for the long-term financial security of a child or adult with a disability. This plan, which has a similar design to the RESP, is expected to be available by the end of 2008.

As with an RESP, earnings generated on contributions are tax exempt while they remain in the plan. Contributions are not tax deductible and not included in income when paid out. All other amounts paid out of the plan are included in the beneficiary's income. Anyone can contribute to an RDSP with the permission of the holder, and contributions are permitted until the end of the year in which the beneficiary reaches 59. Contributions are limited to a lifetime maximum of $200,000 with no annual limit. Payments from an RDSP must commence by the end of the year in which the beneficiary turns 60.

To augment funds in the RDSP the government will contribute, in the form of Canada Disability Savings Grants (CDSG), funds equivalent to between 100 per cent to 300 per cent of RDSP contributions, to a maximum of $3,500 annually, and $70,000 over the lifetime of the beneficiary, depending on the net income of the beneficiary's family. The federal government will also contribute up to $1,000 annually in Canada Disability Savings Bonds (CDSB), to a maximum of $20,000 depending on the beneficiary's family net income. Lower-income families may qualify for payments from the CDSB program without having to make a contribution to an RDSP. Beneficiaries must be 49 years of age or younger at the end of the year to be eligible for a CDSG or CDSB.

If the beneficiary is a minor or has reached the age of majority but is not competent, their parent or certain other individuals can open the RDSP and become its holder.

Only a person who is a resident of Canada and eligible for the disability tax credit (DTC) can be a beneficiary under an RDSP. If the beneficiary's condition improves to the extent they no longer qualify for the DTC, proceeds of the RDSP (less any repayment of CDSGs and CDSBs) must be paid to the beneficiary and the plan collapsed.

## TAX ADVANTAGED INVESTMENTS

The term tax shelter is commonly used when referring to investments and/or other arrangements with tax advantages, but it also has a very specific meaning for tax purposes. The definition is complex, but generally an investment or "gifting arrangement" may be considered a tax shelter under the *Income Tax Act* if:

- it is promoted as offering tax savings; and
- it is reasonable to consider that the losses, deductions or credits resulting from the investment or arrangement would, within the first four years, be equal to or more than the net cost of the original investment.

Taxpayers face a number of limitations with respect to tax shelter deductions and credits. Such deductions and credits can, for instance, result in alternative minimum tax (AMT) (see page 165) or be limited by at-risk rules, which state that individuals may not write off more than the cost of their investment.

Deductions and credits will also be limited if loans related to tax shelters are considered limited-recourse debt, as defined by the *Income Tax Act*.

To avoid being considered limited-recourse debt, money must be borrowed with bona-fide arrangements to repay the principal within 10 years. Interest must be payable regularly at prescribed rates, with the investor at full risk for the loan. Limited recourse debt is not included in the adjusted cost base (ACB) of an investment.

Taxpayers must specifically identify any tax shelter investment deductions or credits, accompanied by a shelter identification number, on their tax return. Tax shelter promoters should provide the necessary filing forms and relevant details, such as the amounts for losses or deductions. An investment or arrangement can be considered a tax shelter even if the promoter has not specifically represented it as a tax shelter or obtained an identification number. However, if an investment or arrangement is found to be a tax shelter and an identification number was not obtained all deductions and claims relating to the tax shelter will be denied.

Tax opinions of accountants and lawyers provided by the promoter of a tax shelter, or the existence of a tax shelter identification number, do not indicate the CRA has confirmed that deductions or credits related to the tax shelter will be allowed. It is common for the CRA to disallow deductions from tax shelters, often going back and reassessing years where it had previously allowed them. Therefore, before you invest in a tax shelter, it may be wise to seek independent tax advice from your Certified General Accountant to assess the potential risks and benefits.

## Tax Tips

Obtain the benefit of tax shelter deductions in advance. Apply to your CRA district taxation office for permission to reduce income taxes at source to reflect tax shelter deductions.

## Limited Partnerships (LP)

Limited partnerships (LP) provide limited liability, while allowing the investor a flow-through of tax losses directly to them. LP investors are taxed on their share of income or loss in the partnership. Cash distributions represent partnership drawings and reduce the limited partner's ACB but do not represent taxable income.

For partnership interests acquired after February 22, 1994, a capital gain must be reported where a limited or passive partner has a negative ACB in their partnership interest at the end of a fiscal period. This provision will prevent tax shelter arrangements where tax-deductible losses are claimed and the investor subsequently receives cash distributions exceeding the partnership interest costs. Only the income or loss for a prior (not the current) period will be taken into account in determining the ACB of a partnership interest.

In addition, losses allocated to a limited partner in a taxation year are restricted to that limited partner's at-risk amount at the end of the fiscal period of the partnership, minus certain other deductions. For most investors, their share of a partnership's losses and their at-risk amount will be the amounts reported on the information slip provided by the partnership.

Matchable expenditures rules introduced in 1996, and further restrictions added in 2001, have eliminated mutual fund and film limited partnership tax shelters. However, grandfathering provisions apply for certain agreements made in writing prior to September 18, 2001. Consult your Certified General Accountant for specific details.

## Rental Real Estate and Real Estate Limited Partnerships

Rental real estate used for commercial purposes might provide taxpayers with the ability to leverage capital, write off expenses, earn CCA-sheltered rental income and enjoy capital appreciation on their investment. Investing in rental real estate through a limited partnership may slightly escalate the rate at which CCA can be claimed because the partnership claims the CCA and the investor deducts the financing costs. If the investor acquired the property directly, the financing costs would increase the rental expenses and potentially reduce the permitted CCA claim.

Rental income received from real estate might, under certain circumstances, be considered by the CRA to be either income from a business or income from property. That is a key distinction because the two are sometimes treated differently from a tax standpoint.

In most cases, rental income will be considered income from property if it is earned by renting space and providing only basic services. If additional services are provided, the rental income may be considered business income. The more services provided, the greater the chance the rental operation is a business. However, as the differences between business and property income are not clearly defined in the *Income Tax Act*, it is best to check with your Certified General Accountant to get clarification.

Expenses incurred to repair or improve a home or a portion thereof, in preparation for or in the course of renting it out, may qualify as either current expenditures or, depending on factors such as the significance and permanence of those improvements, as capital expenditures.

Market considerations aside, some tax aspects associated with rental real estate could potentially reduce its appeal. For example, while CCA in respect of a rental property may be claimed to shelter net rental income from tax, it may not be claimed to create or increase a loss. The fact that when the property is sold any recapture will be added to the investor's income (to the extent proceeds of disposition exceed the undepreciated capital cost) further diminishes the potential advantages of claiming CCA on rental real estate.

If you are a Canadian resident that owns foreign property which is being rented or leased out, consult your Certified General Accountant to help you determine the correct tax treatment and any elections that might be required with respect to that property.

## Tax Tips

Profits and losses from rental property can affect your RRSP deduction limit.

If you are renting out a property that you own, such as a cottage, for a portion of the year, be sure that you keep separate, meticulous records of expenses incurred for personal use and rental use. This will assist you to be able to deduct 100 per cent of rental expenses, as well as a proportion of other fixed costs, like property taxes, against rental income.

# Labour-Sponsored Venture Capital Corporation (LSVCC)

Labour-sponsored venture capital corporations (LSVCC) are investments sponsored by labour organizations that allow individuals to pool their money to purchase a diversified portfolio of small and medium-sized businesses. Taxpayers can register their LSVCC purchase as an RRSP and receive the normal RRSP tax deduction as well as the federal and provincial/territorial tax credits.

The federal government provides a maximum credit of 15 per cent on a $5,000 investment under this program; some provinces also have their own labour-sponsored funds, with varying rules regarding the maximum allowable investment and corresponding provincial credit.

Investments made in an LSVCC in the first 60 days of the year will qualify as contributions for either the previous or current tax year.

LSVCC shares redeemed during the month of February or on March 1 of a calendar year (only up to February 29 during a leap year) are treated as if they had been redeemed 30 days later. This means shareholders who are 30 or fewer days short of holding their investment for the requisite number of years will avoid clawback of the tax credit. They will also have the opportunity to acquire new LSVCC shares during the first 60 days of a year using proceeds from the redemption of existing shares, thereby making them eligible to claim a tax credit for the previous year.

This tax credit does not reduce the ACB of the shares held but will reduce any capital loss realized on their disposition.

To avoid a tax credit clawback, LSVCC investments must be held for at least eight years (five years if they were purchased prior to March 6, 1996). In case of death, the LSVCC can be redeemed immediately, without clawback of the tax credits.

## Tax Tips

If you have a shortage of cash, consider borrowing your RRSP contribution and investing it in an LSVCC. If you were in the highest tax bracket, your tax savings from a maximum allowable federal and provincial/territorial investment could be substantial. You can then use your tax savings to repay most of the loan.

If you own units of an LSVCC purchased in 2000 or earlier, check the terms of your fund. In some cases it may be possible to redeem the units of a fund and reinvest them in the same fund (or another one) to obtain another tax credit. Under federal rules, fund units must be held for a minimum of five years if purchased before March 6, 1996, or eight years if purchased after March 5, 1996. The equivalent provincial and territorial rules vary by jurisdiction. Also, before redeeming your units, be sure and check the terms under the prospectus of the fund you purchased as redemption fees imposed by the fund company may also apply.

## Flow-Through Shares and Oil, Gas and Minerals

Special tax incentives exist to encourage individuals to risk capital for the exploration and development of oil, gas and minerals. These incentives are offered through flow-through shares, joint ventures and limited partnerships. Through such vehicles, individuals may be eligible to deduct specific exploration expenses and other resource-related incentives.

Flow-through shares allow issuing companies to renounce certain deductions in favour of the investor. The initially acquired shares are priced at a premium to market value so the company can participate in the tax savings. Investor deductions generally reduce the cost base of the shares to zero, resulting in a capital gain equal to the entire proceeds when the shares are sold.

In addition to deductions for expenses, there is a 15 per cent non-refundable mineral exploration tax credit available to individuals who invest in qualifying flow-through shares. To be eligible the flow-through share agreement must be made on or before March 31, 2009.

Some provinces have also announced that similar tax credits related to mining activity in their respective jurisdictions will be enacted or extended.

Enhanced tax incentives also exist with respect to the availability of flow-through shares for investors in certain renewable energy and energy conservation projects.

Joint ventures are similar to limited partnerships except that at-risk rules do not apply. Partnerships and joint ventures may also be eligible for additional tax benefits in the form of Alberta royalty tax credits and provincial/territorial crown royalty tax rebate programs.

Consult your Certified General Accountant for details.

## Universal Life (UL) Insurance Policies

Exempt universal life (UL) insurance policies offer many tax advantages. Under a UL policy, for instance:

- premiums paid in excess of the mortality cost and premium tax are accumulated and invested. Income tax on the returns of investments held within the accumulation fund is deferred until withdrawals are made from the policy; and

- when the policyholder dies, beneficiaries generally receive both the face value of the life insurance and full amount of the accumulation fund tax free, resulting in permanent tax savings and partially funding the estate out of pre-tax dollars.

Furthermore, UL can be used to fund retirement needs. Individuals can, for example, borrow from their policy or pledge it as security for a loan, subject to the terms of the policy, with the loan providing a cash flow to fund retirement. Since this cash has resulted from a loan, rather than income, it is not taxable. Also, if repayment of the loan is deferred until the death of the policyholder, the loan will effectively be partially repaid out of pre-tax dollars.

UL insurance is, however, a complex product and should only be purchased with professional advice, including a full explanation of the plan's terms, underlying investments and costs.

### Tax Tips

Don't confuse insurance policy dividends with corporate dividends. Insurance policy dividends are not a distribution of corporate profits; they are a return of premiums and as such are not taxable so long as they do not exceed the insurance policy cost.

# DEFERRED INCOME PLANS

Deferred income plans allow taxpayers to earn investment income on which they can defer paying tax while it remains in the plan. Some deferred income plans also allow a tax deduction, within specified limits, for contributions made.

## Registered Retirement Savings Plans (RRSP)

Registered retirement savings plans (RRSP) are registered plans into which individuals contribute savings or eligible investments for future use — typically, but not necessarily exclusively, for retirement. Taxpayers can have several different RRSPs and invest each in a variety of eligible vehicles, such as guaranteed investment certificates (GIC) or mutual funds.

Eligible RRSP contribution amounts reduce taxpayers' taxable income and thus save tax. However, any RRSP withdrawal will trigger an income inclusion for that taxation year, regardless of whether some — or all — of the amount withdrawn is recontributed to the plan later that year.

105

Taxpayers may be required to pay certain RRSP-related administrative or management fees outside of their plan. Such fees are not tax-deductible, even when paid outside of an RRSP.

## Tax Tips

Contribute to your RRSP early in the year. If, for example, you contribute $20,000 — the maximum annual possible contribution for 2008 — at the beginning of the year instead of at the end, over a 25-year period, assuming an 8 per cent rate of return, you would have an extra $116,970 in your RRSP.

If you are an employee who is making regular RRSP contributions, request that the amount of income tax withheld on your paycheque be reduced in order to reflect the savings those contributions will bring. This is a more efficient way to manage your money than overpaying tax up front, then waiting for a refund the following year.

Individuals with low earned income that precludes their owing any tax should still consider filing a tax return in order to create RRSP contribution room for future use because 18 per cent of earned income from the previous year is eligible to be contributed to an RRSP.

## Registered Retirement Savings Plan Contribution Limits

The annual RRSP contribution limit is 18 per cent of the previous year's earned income to the allowable maximum (see below); less the previous year's pension adjustment (PA) as reported on the T4, plus unused contribution room carried forward from previous years. The PA for a year is a measure of the total value of the benefit earned for the year under a registered pension plan (RPP) or deferred profit sharing plan (DPSP). Past service pension adjustments, if any, are also deducted. The contribution limit also takes into account total pension adjustment reversals (PAR). PARs restore lost contribution room to individuals leaving RPPs or DPSPs before retirement.

The definition of "earned income" includes:

- employment earnings, net of union dues and employment expenses;
- research grants (net of related expenses);
- net income from self-employment and active partnership income;
- disability pensions under the C/QPP;
- royalties;
- net rental income;
- alimony or separation allowances received;
- employee profit sharing plan allocations; and

- supplementary unemployment benefit plan payments (not EI).

Less:

- the current year's loss from self-employment or an active partnership;
- deductible alimony and maintenance payments; and
- current year rental losses.

The maximum annual contribution has been increased to $20,000 in 2008, up from $19,000 in 2007. That ceiling is scheduled to increase after 2008 to at least $21,000 in 2009; and $22,000 in 2010, after which the annual maximum contribution rates will be indexed to reflect increases in average wage growth.

The CRA reports individuals' RRSP contribution limits for the current tax year on the notice of assessment they receive after filing their previous year's tax return. Eligible contributions must be made either during the calendar year or within 60 days of the calendar year end in order to be deductible for the previous tax year. Unused RRSP limits that have accumulated since 1991 are eligible to be carried forward by the taxpayer.

Contributions to a personal RRSP may be made until the end of the calendar year in which the taxpayer turns 71 (up from 69 in 2006).

There is a special provision available for taxpayers who were born in 1937, and originally required to terminate their RRSP in 2006 under the previous age limit of 69. They can elect to convert any proceeds previously transferred to a registered retirement income fund (RRIF) back into an RRSP. However, if they decide to keep those funds in an RRIF, there will be no mandatory minimum withdrawal from that RRIF for taxpayers as they turn 71 in 2008.

## Tax Tips

If you don't have enough cash to top up your RRSP, consider making a contribution in lieu of cash, or "in kind" as it is commonly phrased. The asset transferred must be a qualified investment. These may include publicly listed stocks (and some private company shares if they are held at arm's length), corporate and government bonds, debentures and similar obligations. Be careful when transferring investments that have declined in value, because that loss will not be deductible for tax purposes. Consult your Certified General Accountant for advice.

You don't have to deduct an RRSP contribution the year in which it is made; instead, you can carry it forward for deduction in a future period when you have income placing you in a higher tax bracket. Be sure you have utilized all personal tax credits before deducting your RRSP contribution.

Moreover, amendments will be permitted to existing registered annuity plans established under the previous age rule that belong to taxpayers who turn 71 in 2008.

## Spousal Registered Retirement Savings Plans

Taxpayers can contribute to their own RRSP, a spouse or common-law partner's RRSP, or both provided they do not exceed their maximum deductible amount. Spousal contributions become the spouse/common-law partner's property. Although spousal contributions reduce the contributor's RRSP limit, they don't affect the recipient spouse's contribution limits for their own RRSP.

A spousal RRSP contribution has no more immediate tax benefits than contributing toward a personal RRSP. The future tax savings could be substantial, however. Contributing to spousal RRSPs gives taxpayers and their spouses/common-law partners the opportunity to equalize retirement income and reduce their future tax liability.

If, for instance, one spouse or common-law partner belongs to a good registered pension plan and the other does not, it may be beneficial for the spouse or partner with the pension plan to contribute to a spousal RRSP. Then during retirement, a potential scenario might be for that spouse to draw on their pension and either leave funds in the spousal RRSP or withdraw them in amounts that would be non-taxable or taxed at lower rates.

Contributors should be aware, however, that some or all of the income withdrawn from a spousal plan might be taxable in their hands if spousal contributions were made in either the year of withdrawal or the two preceding years. If, on the other hand, the spouse or common-law partner converts their RRSP to an annuity or a registered retirement income fund (RRIF), withdrawing only the minimum RRIF payment required, there would be no attribution to the contributor.

Contributions to a spousal RRSP may be made until the end of the year in which the spouse or common-law partner turns 71 (up from 69 in 2006), even if the contributor is older than 71.

### Tax Tips

If you have both a regular and a spousal RRSP and are the annuitant for each, you can transfer the proceeds of one plan into the other prior to maturity if you believe that will provide certain advantages, such as administrative ease or a reduction of RRSP fees. The combined new plan would then be classified as a spousal plan.

## Self-Directed Registered Retirement Savings Plans

Investing in an RRSP through banks, trust companies, life insurance companies and mutual funds is usually the most convenient way to start an RRSP. But when the size of an RRSP portfolio and the number of RRSPs an individual owns becomes larger, a self-directed RRSP could allow them more flexibility and control over their investments within their plan. It also provides plan holders an opportunity to consolidate these investments.

The eligible investments are quite extensive and include cash and amounts on deposit with financial institutions (including most GICs), publicly listed and some private company shares, mortgages, bonds and mutual funds.

There used to be a restriction on the percentage of foreign property held inside an RRSP investment portfolio, but that was eliminated by the 2005 federal budget.

---

### Tax Tips

Beware of the tax consequences when transferring investments to your RRSP. The CRA treats such transfers as being similar to a sale of the investment. Moreover, while deemed capital gains triggered by a transfer to an RRSP are taxable, deemed capital losses are not deductible. So instead of transferring a money-losing investment to your RRSP, consider selling it, then contributing the cash to your RRSP and repurchasing the investment within the RRSP. This will lock in or "crystallize" your capital loss.

Be careful that you only place qualified investments into your self-directed RRSP. The *Income Tax Act* imposes a 1 per cent per month penalty tax on the value of non-qualified investments placed into an RRSP.

---

## Special Registered Retirement Savings Plan Contributions

Individuals are allowed to transfer retiring allowances (which may include severance pay and accumulated sick leave credits) directly into their RRSP, within certain limits. For years of service between 1989 and 1995 inclusive, the limit is $2,000 per year. For years prior to 1989, an additional $1,500, for an annual total of $3,500, may be contributed for each year of service that the employee did not have a pension plan.

No special contributions are allowed for years of service from 1996 onwards.

Directly transferring such lump-sum payments to an RRSP will eliminate withholding tax deductions. Individuals who directly receive those lump-sum payments still have 60 days after year end to contribute to their RRSP and obtain a deduction for the year of receipt. They cannot carry forward unused special RRSP contributions to future years. (See Retiring Allowance and Termination Payments, page 40.)

## Creditor-Proofing RRSPs

In the event of bankruptcy, creditors are able to seize funds from most RRSP plans held at financial institutions. However, RRSPs held through an insurance policy that is properly structured in terms of beneficiaries, etc., are generally exempt from creditors under the *Bankruptcy and Insolvency Act*. Therefore, most individuals — particularly if they are self-employed and face a potentially greater risk of bankruptcy — should consider creditor proofing at least a portion of their RRSP portfolio in this fashion. Your Certified General Accountant can help you set this up.

Amendments to the *Bankruptcy and Insolvency Act*, which have received Royal Assent, had not yet come into force when this book was published in 2008. Such amendments would expand this protection to RRSP contributions made more than 12 months prior to bankruptcy. Final details have yet to be worked out. Check with your Certified General Accountant for updates if this is an area of concern.

## RRSP Overcontributions

Overcontributions to an RRSP that are in excess of $2,000 are assessed a penalty of 1 per cent per month. Taxpayers may deduct all or a portion of the excess balance in a subsequent year, provided the deduction amount is within their normal contribution limits for that year. Subsequent deduction of the excess may also occur after the year an individual turns 71 (up from 69 in 2006) or in years after the plan has matured — provided the individual has sufficient contribution room to absorb it.

### Tax Tips

Overcontributions to an RRSP can be designated as a repayment of an outstanding Home Buyers' Plan (HBP) loan. Therefore if you have overcontributed more than $2,000, you can avoid penalties that might otherwise apply by using that amount to pay down an HBP loan.

## RRSP Education Withdrawals

Taxpayers are able to withdraw money from their RRSP for qualifying full-time education and training for either themselves or their spouse/common-law partner, but not both at the same time, on a tax-free basis.

(For individuals with disabilities, this provision covers both full or part-time education and training.)

This provision is known as the Lifelong Learning Plan (LLP).

LLP withdrawals may not exceed $10,000 in a year and $20,000 over a four-year period. Taxpayers can participate in the plan as many times as they wish, but may not start a new plan before the end of the year in which all repayments are made for previous withdrawals. Withdrawals are generally repayable in equal instalments over 10 years, commencing no later than 60 days after the fifth year marking the date of the first withdrawal (or sooner if the student fails to remain in the program full time).

Withdrawals can also be repaid earlier than required. Amounts that are not repaid as scheduled will be added to taxable income.

## Tax Tips

Students in medical residency programs that last for at least three months and qualify for the tuition fee tax credit may also participate in the LLP program.

## Home Buyers' Plan (HBP)

Individuals may withdraw up to $20,000 from their RRSP, without attracting immediate taxation, to assist in acquiring an owner-occupied home. The home must be acquired by October 1 of the year following the withdrawal, which is made using CRA Form T1036.

An ordinary RRSP contribution made less than 90 days before a withdrawal cannot be deducted.

Withdrawn amounts are repayable in equal annual sums over 15 years, beginning no later than the second year following the year of withdrawal (although they can also be made more quickly, if the plan holder is able). Repayments due in a specific year can only be made during that year or within 60 days after the year end. If, during a particular year, an individual does not repay the scheduled amount, or repays only part of it, the unpaid portion will be included in their income for that year.

To participate, prospective homebuyers or their spouse/common-law partners cannot have occupied a home as a principal residence at any time from the beginning of the fourth calendar year before the withdrawal year to 31 days before the withdrawal. Those who wish to withdraw in 2008, for example, must not have owned a home after 2003.

There are special withdrawal rules with respect to purchasing a home for the benefit of a person with a disability who qualifies for the disability tax credit (DTC). These allow for previous home ownership and multiple withdrawals.

Individuals who qualify for the DTC, as well as relatives helping to support them, can temporarily withdraw up to $20,000 from their RRSP without tax penalty, provided such funds are used to support the acquisition of a dwelling that is either more accessible for the individual with a disability, or better suited to their care.

This provision will apply, even if the individual with a disability or their relative has participated in the HBP program in the past, provided all outstanding amounts withdrawn from any previous participation have been repaid within the 15-year allowable maximum.

## Registered Retirement Income Funds (RRIF), Annuities and Retirement Options

Individuals are required to terminate their RRSP plans by the end of the year during which they turn 71 (up from age 69 in 2006). When terminating an RRSP, there are three alternatives to choose from. Plan holders may:

- withdraw the funds, in which case the total amount withdrawn is included in their annual income;

- purchase an annuity that provides a regular income for a defined period that may include their lifetime; the joint lifetime of both they and their spouse/common-law partner; a fixed period; or combinations thereof. The annuity payments will be taxed as received; or

- transfer an RRSP into a registered retirement income fund (RRIF), which is similar to an RRSP in that the plans' funds and income earned remain untaxed until withdrawn. Although the funds are held in a trust, taxpayers may continue to exercise authority over investment decisions. They must withdraw a minimum amount from the plan each year, based on their age or that of a younger spouse/common-law partner, upon which they are then taxed. The minimum withdrawal amount increases each year until age 94 when it becomes fixed at 20 per cent annually until the plan is depleted.

Within an RRIF, individuals also have the option of withdrawing amounts in excess of the minimum although any excess withdrawn amounts will also become taxable in that year.

## Registered Pension Plans (RPP)

In addition to having an RRSP, many employees also belong to a registered pension plan (RPP) through their employer.

The maximum allowable contribution for a money purchase RPP has been increased to $21,000 in 2008 (from $20,000 in 2007) and, in future, will increase again to at least $22,000 in 2009, after which they will be indexed annually to account for the average wage growth.

Annual money purchase plan RPP contribution limits are 18 per cent of pensionable earnings (the same as with RRSPs), up to the limits stated above.

The maximum pension limit for defined-benefit registered pension plans (RPP) increased to $2,333 in 2008 from $2,222 in 2007; they will increase again to at least $2,444 in 2009, after which they will be indexed on an annual basis to reflect increases in average wage growth.

The age limit at which contributors must stop contributing to an RPP is 71 (up from 69 in 2006 and prior years).

Money purchase RPP proceeds are allowed to pay out pension benefits using the same income stream permitted under an RRIF (i.e., minimum payments beginning no later than age 72).

## Other Registered Pension Plan Features

Deductions for RPP contributions, in respect of both current and past services rendered after 1989, are allowed during the year the contribution was made, provided the contribution was made in accordance with the plan's registered terms. This applies whether contributions are mandatory or optional.

The deduction amount for past service contributions rendered before 1990 depends on whether or not taxpayers contributed to any RPP in the year to which the past service applies. If they were not a contributor during that period, they may account for $3,500 times the number of years of eligible service; however, the maximum amount deductible in any one calendar year is only $3,500.

For years of service during which the employee was a contributor, the maximum available deduction is also $3,500, reduced by any current year or past deductions (including those claimed for prior years while not a contributor to any RPP).

Any remaining balance may be carried forward for deduction in subsequent years provided the taxpayer has the available contribution room.

Individuals who make past service contributions to their RPP in instalments will probably pay accrued interest charges. The interest paid for years after 1989 is considered a past service contribution.

Within limitations, the *Income Tax Act* provides for the transfer of benefits accrued under a defined-benefit RPP to either a money purchase RPP, RRSP or RRIF. Likewise, the proceeds of a money purchase pension plan can be transferred to another money purchase RPP, RRSP or RRIF.

Furthermore, funds previously transferred from a money purchase RPP into an RRSP or RRIF can be transferred back into the money purchase pension plan, where they are subject to the same payout requirement as the RRIF.

An employee may also deduct, within limits, additional voluntary contributions (AVC) under a money purchase plan. The amount deducted will, however, affect their RRSP limit the following year.

The CRA now recognizes registered pension plans that provide survivor benefits to same-sex partners.

Beginning in 2008, certain defined benefit pension plan holders who are at least 55 years of age may now receive up to 60 per cent of their pension, while still being permitted to accrue further benefits.

## Individual Pension Plans (IPP)

Another retirement option for certain older, high-income individuals such as managers of owner-operated businesses and corporate executives who have consistently been able to contribute the maximum amount to their RRSP on an annual basis might be an Individual Pension Plan (IPP). The annual contribution amount to an IPP, which is a defined benefit plan, depends on an actuarial calculation which determines how much is required to fund a pre-established pension amount. This minimum amount increases with age.

IPP funds are used to fund retirement through various options, including the owner withdrawing a prescribed annual pension amount, transferring the commuted value of accrued pension benefits to a locked-in plan, or purchasing a fixed value annuity; the taxpayer's spouse might also be eligible to receive an annuity if they are a survivor.

Although the IPP does not have a restricted ceiling for annual contributions as does an RRSP, some of the logistics associated with IPPs are similar to RRSPs in that the contributor gets a tax deduction for their contribution amount; and the invested funds are allowed to grow on a tax-deferred basis until they are ultimately withdrawn. Like an RPP, IPP contributions create a pension adjustment amount.

The IPP is also generally creditor proof.

Talk to your Certified General Accountant if you think this retirement instrument, which has very complex rules with respect to issues such as the treatment of surplus amounts, transfer of plan assets to another retirement fund and disposition of proceeds upon death, among others, might be beneficial to you.

## Locked-In Accounts

When individuals leave their place of employment, they often have the option of either receiving a pension at retirement or transferring the commuted value of their deferred pension. Pension legislation requires that the commuted value cannot be paid to the individual employees, but must instead be either transferred directly to another pension plan or locked-in plan, or used to purchase a life annuity.

Locked-in plans are just RRSPs or RRIFs with an extra layer of rules found in pension benefits legislation. The federal government and the provinces (except P.E.I.) each have their own pension benefits legislation and hence the requirements for locked-in plans vary by jurisdiction. Locked-in plans are governed by legislation affecting the pension plan from where the funds originate, which might not necessarily be the jurisdiction where an individual currently resides. Locked-in plans should not be confused with a fixed-term investment inside an RRSP, such as a GIC.

In Ontario, for instance, the commuted value of a pension may be transferred to a locked-in retirement account (LIRA). Unlike a regular RRSP, withdrawals can only be made from a LIRA in very limited circumstances. At retirement — which can generally occur as early as 55 or as late as 71 — the LIRA funds must be transferred to a locked-in retirement income plan, or used to purchase a life annuity. In Ontario such plans are known as life-income funds (LIF) or locked-in retirement income funds (LRIF). LIFs and LRIFs are subject to the same annual minimum withdrawal limits as RRIFs and also to maximum withdrawal limits determined by pension legislation.

There are important differences between various types of locked-in plans, as well as between plans listed under the same name that are governed by the legislation of different jurisdictions. Consult your plan administrator to help you sort this all out.

In May 2008, the federal Minister of Finance announced that major changes with respect to federally regulated locked-in plans were in effect. Taxpayers who are at least 55 years of age are now entitled to transfer locked-in assets to a restricted life income fund (RLIF). RLIFs allow for the conversion of up to 50 per cent of the plan's holdings into an unlocked tax-deferred savings vehicle. This will be a one-time opportunity at the time of creation of the RLIF, and must be exercised within 60 days.

Individuals who are at least 55 years of age, with up to a combined total of $22,450 in 2008 in federally regulated LIFs, locked-in RRSPs, RLIFs or RLSPs can also wind up the LIF, RLIF, or RLSP accounts (but not the locked-in RRSP), or convert them to a tax-deferred savings vehicle such as an RRSP or RRIF.

Furthermore, all individuals — regardless of age — who are facing financial hardship as a result of circumstances that involve low income ($33,675 in 2008), or high disability or medical-related costs relative to their income (20 per cent or greater), will be entitled to withdraw up to $22,450 in 2008 from any combination of federally regulated LIFs, locked-in RRSPs, RLIFs or RLSPs within a 30-day period.

The $22,450 threshold in 2008 is scheduled to rise in subsequent years in line with the average industrial wage.

If the taxpayer has a spouse, they must also formally approve the type of transfer and/or withdrawal from locked-in-funds based on the three options available.

Under federal law, extraordinary withdrawals in circumstances involving reduced life expectancy or a situation where a taxpayer leaves Canada permanently are also permitted under LIF, locked-in RRSP, RLIF and RLSP contracts.

## Tax-Free Savings Account (TFSA)

The 2008 federal budget introduced a new Tax-Free Savings Account (TFSA) which will come into effect January 1, 2009.

The TFSA will allow Canadians who are 18 and older to save up to $5,000 per year — an amount that will be indexed to inflation in future years, and rounded to the nearest $500. Unlike an RRSP, investors will not be able to deduct contributions — made in after-tax dollars — to a TFSA for tax purposes; however investment income, including capital gains earned within the TFSA, will not be subject to tax, even when the funds are ultimately withdrawn.

Unused contribution room in a TFSA will carry forward indefinitely to future years. Qualified arm's-length investments that can be held inside the TFSA will, generally speaking, mirror those allowed within RRSPs.

TFSA funds will be permitted to be withdrawn at any time, in any amount, and for any reason without affecting taxable income or eligibility for federal means-tested benefits or tax credits. Furthermore, withdrawn funds can be reinvested back into the TFSA without affecting future contribution room. Spouses may also contribute to a TFSA without having the interest earned from that contribution subject to attribution rules. TFSA assets can also be transferred to a spouse's TFSA upon death.

A TFSA may be carried by the holder indefinitely; there is no time limit to close this account.

Excess contributions to a TFSA will be subject to a tax of 1 per cent per month.

# PART THREE: TAX CREDITS AND RELATED ITEMS

## FEDERAL AND PROVINCIAL/TERRITORIAL NON-REFUNDABLE TAX CREDITS

Federal tax credits reduce the amount of basic federal tax payable. In addition, each of Canada's provinces and territories has its own independent tax structure, with rates that apply to these credits and help further reduce the overall tax payable.

The federal credit is determined by multiplying a gross dollar amount by the lowest federal tax rate, currently 15 per cent for 2008. The gross amount of most tax credits, such as the basic personal, age and spousal credits, are indexed annually by a formula that takes into account increases in the consumer price index (CPI).

Some provinces and territories also index selected non-refundable tax credits based on their own CPI formula. Generally speaking, a taxpayer is deemed to be resident of a province or territory if they reside in that jurisdiction on December 31 of a particular tax year. Where they have ties to more than one jurisdiction, the courts generally side with the province or territory to which they have the most significant residential connection.

Unused federal and provincial tax credits are non-refundable.

For a summary of federal and provincial/territorial tax credits, see Appendix I, page 179.

## Basic Personal Credit

Federally, taxpayers are, in 2008, entitled to claim the basic personal credit of 15 per cent on $9,600, for a credit of $1,440 (the same as in 2007, due to increases announced in late 2007 in the Minister of Finance's Economic Statement).

Provincially, the corresponding figures are:

**Alberta:** Alberta taxpayers are entitled to claim a basic personal credit of 10 per cent on $16,161, or $1,616 (up from $15,435, or $1,544 in 2007).

**British Columbia:** British Columbia taxpayers are entitled to claim a basic personal credit of 5.06 per cent on $9,189, or $465 (up from $9,027, or $515 on a credit of 5.70 per cent in 2007).

**Manitoba:** Manitoba taxpayers are entitled to claim a basic personal credit of 10.90 per cent on $8,034, or $876 (up from $7,834, or $854 in 2007).

**New Brunswick:** New Brunswick taxpayers are entitled to claim a basic personal credit of 10.12 per cent on $8,395, or $850 (up from $8,239, or $834 in 2007).

**Newfoundland and Labrador:** Newfoundland and Labrador taxpayers may claim an average personal credit of 8.20 per cent on $7,566, or $620 in 2008 (up from $7,484, or $721 based on an average personal credit of 9.64 per cent in 2007).

**Northwest Territories:** Northwest Territories taxpayers are entitled to claim a basic personal credit of 5.90 per cent on $12,355, or $729 (up from $12,125, or $715 in 2007).

**Nova Scotia:** Nova Scotia taxpayers are entitled to claim a basic personal credit of 8.79 per cent on $7,731, or $680 (up from $7,481, or $658 in 2007).

**Nunavut:** Nunavut taxpayers are entitled to claim a basic personal credit of 4 per cent on $11,360, or $454 (up from $11,149, or $446 in 2007).

**Ontario:** Ontario taxpayers are entitled to claim a basic personal credit of 6.05 per cent on $8,681, or $525 (up from $8,553, or $517 in 2007).

**Prince Edward Island:** Prince Edward Island taxpayers are entitled to claim a basic personal credit of 9.80 per cent on $7,708, or $755 in 2008 (up from an average credit of $7,560, or $741 in 2007).

**Quebec:** Quebec taxpayers are entitled to claim a basic personal credit of 20 per cent on $10,215, or $2,043 (see explanation in Appendix I).

**Saskatchewan:** Saskatchewan taxpayers are entitled to claim a basic personal credit of 11 per cent on $12,945, or $1,424 (up from $8,778, or $966 in 2007).

**Yukon:** Yukon taxpayers are entitled to claim a basic personal credit of 7.04 per cent on $9,600, or $676 (no change from 2007).

## The Canada Employment Credit

The Canada Employment Credit is available on 15 per cent of $1,019, for a credit of $153 in 2008 (up from $1,000, or $150 in 2007).

The Yukon Territory has matched this federal credit, which is available on 7.04 per cent of $1,019 for a credit of $72.

## Spousal Credit

Individuals supporting a spouse or common-law partner whose net income is less than $9,600 (the same as in 2007, due to increases announced in the Minister's 2007 Economic Statement) may claim the federal spousal credit. They may claim the maximum credit of 15 per cent on $9,600, for a credit of $1,440, if the spouse or common-law partner's income is nil. That credit is reduced if the spouse or common-law partner's net income is more than nil but less than $9,600, where the credit is eliminated.

Provincially, the corresponding figures are as follows:

**Alberta:** Alberta taxpayers supporting a spouse or common-law partner whose net income is less than $16,161 (compared to $15,435 in 2007) may claim the spousal credit. They may claim the maximum credit of 10 per cent on $16,161, or $1,616, if the spouse or common-law partner's income is nil. That credit is reduced if the spouse or common-law partner's net income is more than nil but less than $16,161, where the credit is eliminated.

**British Columbia:** British Columbia taxpayers supporting a spouse or common-law partner whose net income is less than $8,655 (compared to $8,502, based on a credit of 5.70 per cent in 2007) may claim the spousal credit. They may claim the maximum credit at a new rate of 5.06 per cent on $7,868, or $398, if the spouse or common-law partner's income is $787 or less (compared to $773 in 2007). That credit is reduced if the spouse or common-law partner's net income is more than $787 but less than $8,655, where the credit is eliminated.

**Manitoba:** Manitoba taxpayers supporting a spouse or common-law partner whose net income is less than $8,034 (compared to $7,131 in 2007) may claim the spousal credit. They may claim the maximum credit of 10.90 per cent on $8,034, or $876, if the spouse or common-law partner's income is nil (compared to $649 in 2007, a limit that has since been eliminated). That credit is reduced if the spouse or common-law partner's net income is more than nil but less than $8,034, where the credit is eliminated.

**New Brunswick:** New Brunswick taxpayers supporting a spouse or common-law partner whose net income is less than $7,842 (compared to $7,696 in 2007) may claim the spousal credit. They may claim the maximum credit of 10.12 per cent on $7,129, or $721, if the spouse or common-law partner's income is $713 or less (compared to $700 in 2007). That credit is reduced if the spouse or common-law partner's net income is more than $713 but less than $7,842, where the credit is eliminated.

**Newfoundland and Labrador:** Newfoundland and Labrador taxpayers supporting a spouse or common-law partner whose net income is less than $6,802 (up from $6,728, based on an average credit of 9.64 per cent in 2007) may claim the spousal credit. For 2008, they may claim an average maximum credit of 8.20 per cent on $6,183, or $507, if the spouse or common-law partner's income is $619 or less (up from $612 in 2007). That credit is reduced if the spouse or common-law partner's net income is more than $619 but less than $6,802, where the credit is eliminated.

**Northwest Territories:** Northwest Territories taxpayers supporting a spouse or common-law partner whose net income is less than $12,355 (up from $12,125 in 2007) may claim the spousal credit. They may claim the maximum credit of 5.90 per cent on $12,355, or $729, if the spouse or common-law partner's income is nil. That credit is reduced if the spouse or common-law partner's net income is more than nil but less than $12,355, where the credit is eliminated.

**Nova Scotia:** Nova Scotia taxpayers supporting a spouse or common-law partner whose net income is less than $7,221 (up from $6,987 in 2007) may claim the spousal credit. They may claim the maximum credit of 8.79 per cent on $6,565, or $577, if the spouse or common-law partner's income is $656 or less (up from $635 in 2007). That credit is reduced if the spouse or common-law partner's net income is more than $656 but less than $7,221, where the credit is eliminated.

**Nunavut:** Nunavut taxpayers supporting a spouse or common-law partner whose net income is less than $11,360 (up from $11,149 in 2007) may claim the spousal credit. They may claim the maximum credit of 4 per cent on $11,360, or $454, if the spouse or common-law partner's income is nil. That credit is reduced if the spouse or common-law partner's net income is more than nil but less than $11,360, where the credit is eliminated.

**Ontario:** Ontario taxpayers supporting a spouse or common-law partner whose net income is less than $8,108 (compared to $7,988 in 2007) may claim the spousal credit. They may claim the maximum credit of 6.05 per cent on $7,371, or $446, if the spouse or common-law partner's income is $737 or less (compared to $726 in 2007). That credit is reduced if the spouse or common-law partner's net income is more than $737 but less than $8,108, where the credit is eliminated.

**Prince Edward Island:** Prince Edward Island taxpayers supporting a spouse or common-law partner whose net income is less than $7,201 (up from an average of $7,062 in 2007) may claim the spousal credit. They may claim 9.80 per cent on $6,546, or $642, if the spouse or common-law partner's income is $655 or less (up from $642 in 2007). That credit is reduced if the spouse or common-law partner's net income is more than $655 but less than $7,201, where the credit is eliminated.

**Quebec:** Quebec replaced its tax credit for spouses in 2003 with a mechanism for the transfer of the unused portion of non-refundable tax credits from one spouse to another.

*Dependants Credit*

Since 2005, Quebec's tax system grants a refundable tax credit for child assistance. This credit replaces family allowances, non-refundable tax credits for dependent children under age 18 and for the first child of single-parent families, and the tax reduction for families. It is paid quarterly.

For the 2008 taxation year, the maximum amount is equivalent to the total of the following amounts:

| | |
|---|---|
| First child | $2,116 |
| Second and third children | 1,058 |
| Fourth and subsequent children | 1,586 |
| Single-parent family supplement | 741 |

This credit is reduced by 4 per cent for each dollar of the individual's family income in excess of $43,654 if the individual has a qualified spouse, or for $31,984 in other cases.

However, the child assistance payment an individual receives can, in no case, be less than the minimum amount established for him/her. This minimum amount is equal to the total of the following amounts:

| | |
|---|---|
| First child | $594 |
| Second and subsequent children | 548 |
| Single-parent | 297 |

Furthermore, if an individual has a handicapped child, a supplement is added to the child assistance payment to which the individual is entitled. This handicapped child supplement corresponds to $167 per month for each handicapped child, regardless of family income.

The tax system also grants a non-refundable tax credit to a taxpayer with one or more dependent children under age 18 and engaged in certain full-time secondary vocational or post-secondary studies. This tax credit is calculated on the basis of an amount of recognized essential needs of $1,885 per completed term (to a maximum of two terms), that must be reduced by 80 per cent of the child's income for the year, determined regardless of the scholarships, fellowships and awards the student received during the year that gave rise to a deduction in calculating his or her taxable income. The amount obtained is then converted into a tax credit at the rate of 20 per cent.

In 2007, the tax credit claimed by parents for an adult child who is a student — the basic amount for adult children who are students and the amount for children engaged in vocational and post-secondary studies — was replaced by a transfer to parents of the unused portion of the amount for recognized essential needs of the child (to a maximum of $6,730 in 2008).

The tax system also grants a non-refundable tax credit to a taxpayer with one or more adult dependants who are not engaged in certain full-time secondary vocational or post-secondary studies. This tax credit is calculated on the basis of an amount of recognized essential needs of $2,740 that must be reduced by 80 per cent of the dependant's income for the year. This amount is determined regardless of the scholarships, fellowships and awards the dependant received during the year which gave rise to a deduction in calculating his or her taxable income. The amount obtained is then converted into a tax credit at the rate of 20 per cent.

*Person Living Alone Credit*

The allowable amount for a person living alone is $1,195. Where an individual lived with an adult child who has completed, during that year, at least one recognized term of eligible secondary vocational or post-secondary studies, that person may add $1,485 for a single-parent family to the allowable amount for a person living alone if, for the last month of the year or on the date of his or her death, the individual had no child for whom he or she was entitled to a refundable tax credit for child assistance.

The amount for a person living alone is then combined with the amount for retirement income and the amount with respect to age. The combined amount is reduced at the rate of 15 per cent for each dollar of the taxpayer's net family income in excess of $29,645. The net total is then converted into a tax credit at the rate of 20 per cent.

**Saskatchewan:** Saskatchewan taxpayers supporting a spouse or common-law partner whose net income is less than $13,840 (compared to $9,656 in 2007) may claim the spousal credit. They may claim the maximum credit of 11 per cent on $12,945, or $1,424, if the spouse or common-law partner's income is $895 or less (compared to $878 in 2007). That credit is reduced if the spouse or common-law partner's net income is more than $895 but less than $13,840, where the credit is eliminated.

**Yukon:** Yukon taxpayers supporting a spouse or common-law partner whose net income is less than $9,600 (the same as in 2007) may claim the spousal credit. They may claim the maximum credit of 7.04 per cent on $9,600, or $676, if the spouse or common-law partner's income is nil. That credit is reduced if the spouse or common-law partner's net income is more than nil but less than $9,600, where the credit is eliminated.

Special rules may apply to an individual's claim if their status changed during the year.

## Tax Tips

You may claim an amount for your dependent spouse or common-law partner even if he or she did not live in Canada during the year. To do so, you must supply proof of that support, such as a cancelled cheque or money order receipt, etc., in the name of the eligible payee. The documents submitted should also contain detailed information, such as the recipient's name, address and date of transfer.

If you lived separate and apart from your spouse for all or any part of a year for reasons other than a marriage breakdown, you may still be entitled to claim the spousal credit.

# Equivalent-to-Spouse Credit

Taxpayers may claim the equivalent-to-spouse credit if at any time during the year they were single, divorced or separated and supported a qualified relative, including a child, who lived with and was dependent on them. The equivalent-to-spouse credit is calculated in the same manner as the spousal credit, except in Quebec, where different rules apply (see above).

The following restrictions apply:

- the dependant, other than a child, must be a Canadian resident;
- a dependant child must be either under 18 at any time in the year, or any age if dependent by reason of mental or physical infirmity;
- the claim may only be made in respect of one eligible dependant at a time;
- where two or more individuals are otherwise entitled to a credit in respect of the same person, only one is able to claim the credit; and
- the credit cannot be claimed for an individual on behalf of whom the taxpayer is required to pay a support amount.

To qualify, the dependant need not have lived with or been supported by the taxpayer throughout the entire year.

In Prince Edward Island, the equivalent-to-spouse amount that can be claimed is different than the amount that can be claimed for a spouse or common-law partner. Prince Edward Island taxpayers may claim an eligible individual whose net income is less than $6,923 (the same as in 2007). They may claim a maximum credit of 9.80 per cent on $6,294, or $617, if the equivalent-to-spouse's income is $629 or less (the same as in 2007). That credit is reduced if the spouse or common-law partner's net income is more than $629 but less than $6,923, where the credit is eliminated.

## Tax Tips

If you were entitled to the equivalent-to-spouse claim at the beginning of the year you maintain that entitlement for the full year. Even if you marry during the year, that entitlement remains, provided you don't claim the spousal credit.

If more than one person is eligible to claim this credit on behalf of another individual, such as their child, it is important that a formal agreement be reached as to which taxpayer will do so; otherwise nobody will be able to claim it.

# Age Credit

Individuals age 65 or older in the year are entitled to a federal credit of 15 per cent on $5,276, or $791. This gross amount is reduced by 15 per cent of net income over $31,524, thereby eliminating the entire credit when income of $66,697 is attained.

**Alberta:** Alberta taxpayers 65 or older are entitled to a credit of 10 per cent on $4,503, or $450. The gross amount is reduced by 15 per cent of net income over $33,525, thereby eliminating the entire credit when income of $63,545 is attained.

**British Columbia:** British Columbia taxpayers 65 or older are entitled to a credit of 5.06 per cent on $4,121, or $209. The gross amount is reduced by 15 per cent of net income over $30,674, thereby eliminating the entire credit when income of $58,147 is attained.

**Manitoba:** Manitoba taxpayers 65 or older are entitled to a credit of 10.90 per cent on $3,728, or $406. The gross amount is reduced by 15 per cent of net income over $27,749, thereby eliminating the entire credit when income of $52,602 is attained.

**New Brunswick:** New Brunswick taxpayers 65 or older are entitled to a credit of 10.12 per cent on $4,099, or $415. The gross amount is reduced by 15 per cent of net income over $30,517, thereby eliminating the entire credit when income of $57,844 is attained.

**Newfoundland and Labrador:** Newfoundland and Labrador taxpayers 65 or older are entitled to an average credit in 2008 of 8.20 per cent on $3,556, or $292. The gross amount is reduced by 15 per cent of net income over an average amount of $26,468, thereby eliminating the entire credit when average income of $50,175 is attained.

**Northwest Territories:** Northwest Territories taxpayers 65 or older are entitled to a credit of 5.90 per cent on $6,044, or $357. The gross amount is reduced by 15 per cent of net income over $31,524, thereby eliminating the entire credit when income of $71,817 is attained.

**Nova Scotia:** Nova Scotia taxpayers 65 or older are entitled to a credit of 8.79 per cent on $3,775, or $332. The gross amount is reduced by 15 per cent of net income over $28,101, thereby eliminating the entire credit when income of $53,268 is attained.

**Nunavut:** Nunavut taxpayers 65 or older are entitled to a credit of 4 per cent on $8,520, or $341. The gross amount is reduced by 15 per cent of net income over $31,524, thereby eliminating the entire credit when income of $88,324 is attained.

**Ontario:** Ontario taxpayers 65 or older are entitled to a credit of 6.05 per cent on $4,239, or $256. The gross amount is reduced by 15 per cent of net income over $31,554, thereby eliminating the entire credit when income of $59,814 is attained.

**Prince Edward Island:** Prince Edward Island taxpayers 65 or older are entitled to a credit of 9.80 per cent on $3,764, or $369. The gross amount is reduced by 15 per cent of net income over $28,019, thereby eliminating the entire credit when income of $53,112 is attained.

**Quebec:** Quebec taxpayers 65 or older are entitled to a credit of 20 per cent on $2,200, or $440.

As noted above, this $2,200 amount is then added to the amount for retirement income, and the amount for a person living alone, with the corresponding amounts, as the case may be, of which the individual's spouse may take advantage. The combined total is reduced by 15 per cent of net family income in excess of $29,645. The total of these reduced amounts is then converted to a tax credit at the rate of 20 per cent.

**Saskatchewan:** Saskatchewan taxpayers 65 or older are entitled to a credit of 11 per cent on $4,235, or $466. The gross amount is reduced by 15 per cent of net income over $31,524, thereby eliminating the entire credit when income of $59,757 is attained.

Saskatchewan residents over the age of 64 also qualify for a senior supplementary amount of $1,118, for a credit of $123, regardless of their net income.

**Yukon:** Yukon taxpayers 65 or older are entitled to a credit of 7.04 per cent on $5,276, or $371. The gross amount is reduced by 15 per cent of net income over $31,524, thereby eliminating the entire credit when income of $66,697 is attained.

### Tax Tips

You may be able to claim the unused portion of your spouse or common-law partner's age credit.

## Disability Credit

A 15 per cent federal credit on $7,021, or $1,053, is available to any individual whom a Canadian medical doctor certifies on Form T2201 is suffering from severe and prolonged mental or physical impairment. Once Form T2201 is on file with the CRA, it doesn't need to be resubmitted annually.

**Alberta:** The Alberta provincial portion of this credit is 10 per cent on $12,466, or $1,247.

**British Columbia:** The British Columbia provincial portion of this credit is 5.06 per cent on $6,892, or $349.

**Manitoba:** The Manitoba provincial portion of this credit is 10.90 per cent on $6,180, or $674.

**New Brunswick:** The New Brunswick provincial portion of this credit is 10.12 per cent on $6,797, or $688.

**Newfoundland and Labrador:** The Newfoundland and Labrador provincial portion of this credit for 2008 is an average credit of 8.20 per cent on $5,106, or $419.

**Northwest Territories:** The Northwest Territories territorial portion of this credit is 5.90 per cent on $10,020, or $591.

**Nova Scotia:** The Nova Scotia provincial portion of this credit is 8.79 per cent on $4,596, or $404.

**Nunavut:** The Nunavut territorial portion of this credit is 4 per cent on $11,360, or $454.

**Ontario:** The Ontario provincial portion of this credit is 6.05 per cent on $7,014, or $424.

**Prince Edward Island:** The Prince Edward Island provincial portion of this credit is 9.80 per cent on $6,890, or $675.

**Quebec:** The Quebec provincial portion of this credit is 20 per cent on $2,325, or $465.

**Saskatchewan:** The Saskatchewan provincial portion of this credit is 11 per cent on $8,190, or $901.

**Yukon:** The Yukon territorial portion of this credit is 7.04 per cent on $7,021, or $494.

Other professionals may also certify specific disabilities. For instance, an optometrist can certify sight impairment or an audiologist can certify an individual's hearing disability. Occupational therapists and psychologists can also certify a taxpayer's physical or mental disability, respectively.

This impairment is considered severe if the disability markedly restricts the person in physical daily-living activities, such as walking, speaking, feeding or dressing, or mental activities, such as perceiving, thinking and remembering, among others; and prolonged if the disability lasts, or is expected to last, for a continuous period of at least 12 months. The courts have also often taken a compassionate, common sense approach towards defining whether a person is restricted in their activities of daily living and, in so doing, have considered the overall impact that a disability has had on their lives.

In 2002, for instance, the Tax Court of Canada ruled that although an individual suffering from chronic fatigue syndrome was not markedly restricted from performing any one of the CRA's specified basic activities of daily living, she nevertheless qualified for the credit because of the cumulative restrictive effects that illness had on her ability to function.

The disability tax credit (DTC) also extends to individuals that have been certified by a medical doctor to require therapy at least three times a week, averaging a total of at least 14 hours, to deal with a marked restriction in their ability to perform a basic activity of daily living.

---

## Tax Tips

If you qualify for Canada Pension Plan (CPP) disability benefits, don't forget to check and see whether you also qualify for the DTC.

---

## Disability Tax Credit Supplement

A federal DTC supplement of up to $614 (15 per cent of $4,095) is also available for caregivers of children under 18 who have severe disabilities that require full-time home care. Annual child care and attendant care expenses in excess of $2,399 claimed on behalf of that child will reduce this supplement, eliminating it completely once such expenses reach $6,494.

Provincially, the DTC supplements are as follows:

**Alberta:** For Alberta taxpayers, the maximum DTC supplement is $936 (10 per cent of $9,355). Annual child care and attendant care expenses in excess of $2,552 claimed on behalf of that child will reduce this supplement, eliminating it completely once such expenses reach $11,907.

**British Columbia:** For British Columbia taxpayers, the maximum DTC supplement is $203 (5.06 per cent of $4,021). Annual child care and attendant care expenses in excess of $2,334 claimed on behalf of that child will reduce this supplement, eliminating it completely once such expenses reach $6,355.

**Manitoba:** For Manitoba taxpayers, the maximum DTC supplement is $393 (10.90 per cent of $3,605). Annual child care and attendant care expenses in excess of $2,112 claimed on behalf of that child will reduce this supplement, eliminating it completely once such expenses reach $5,717.

**New Brunswick:** For New Brunswick taxpayers, the maximum DTC supplement is $401 (10.12 per cent of $3,965). Annual child care and attendant care expenses in excess of $2,321 claimed on behalf of that child will reduce this supplement, eliminating it completely once such expenses reach $6,286.

**Newfoundland and Labrador:** For the taxpayers of Newfoundland and Labrador, the maximum DTC supplement is $197 (based on an average of 8.20 per cent of $2,402). Annual child care and attendant care expenses in excess of $2,042 claimed on behalf of that child will reduce this supplement, eliminating it completely once such expenses reach $4,444.

**Northwest Territories:** For taxpayers of the Northwest Territories, the maximum DTC supplement is $242 (5.90 per cent of $4,095). Annual child care and attendant care expenses in excess of $2,399 claimed on behalf of that child will reduce this supplement, eliminating it completely once such expenses reach $6,494.

**Nova Scotia:** For Nova Scotia taxpayers, the maximum DTC supplement is $276 (8.79 per cent of $3,145). Annual child care and attendant care expenses in excess of $2,139 claimed on behalf of that child will reduce this supplement, eliminating it completely once such expenses reach $5,284.

**Nunavut:** For Nunavut taxpayers, the maximum DTC supplement is $164 (4 per cent of $4,095). Annual child care and attendant care expenses in excess of $2,399 claimed on behalf of that child will reduce this supplement, eliminating it completely once such expenses reach $6,494.

**Ontario:** For Ontario taxpayers, the maximum DTC supplement is $248 (6.05 per cent of $4,091). Annual child care and attendant care expenses in excess of $2,396 claimed on behalf of that child will reduce this supplement, eliminating it completely once such expenses reach $6,487.

**Prince Edward Island:** For taxpayers of Prince Edward Island, the maximum DTC supplement is $394 (9.80 per cent of $4,019). Annual child care and attendant care expenses in excess of $2,354 claimed on behalf of that child will reduce this supplement, eliminating it completely once such expenses reach $6,373.

**Quebec:** Not applicable.

**Saskatchewan:** For Saskatchewan taxpayers, the maximum DTC supplement is $901 (11 per cent of $8,190). Annual child care and attendant care expenses in excess of $2,399 claimed on behalf of that child will reduce this supplement, eliminating it completely once such expenses reach $10,589.

**Yukon:** For taxpayers of the Yukon, the maximum DTC supplement is $288 (7.04 per cent of $4,095). Annual child care and attendant care expenses in excess of $2,399 claimed on behalf of that child will reduce this supplement, eliminating it completely once such expenses reach $6,494.

## Child Disability Benefit

A federal child disability benefit (CDB) was introduced in the 2003 federal budget for the benefit of parents whose children qualify for the disability tax credit. For additional details about the CDB, see page 163 in the chapter on Additional Tax Considerations.

## Child Tax Credit

The federal budget of 2007 introduced an annual non-refundable child tax credit, effective January 1, 2007, that pays parents $2,000 for each child under the age of 18 at the end of a taxation year. In 2008, this federal credit is 15 per cent of $2,038, or $306 per child.

The Yukon Territory matched that provision in 2007; the 2008 federal credit there is 7.04 per cent of $2,038, or $143 per child.

Saskatchewan also offers a child amount supplement tax credit of $527 (11 per cent of $4,795). That was available prior to the introduction of the federal credit.

When a child resides with both parents throughout the year, either parent may claim this credit, with any unused portion being transferable between spouses or common-law partners. In instances where a child does not reside with both parents, the parent eligible to make that claim will be the one who is also eligible to claim the wholly dependent person credit in respect of that child. This credit cannot be claimed on behalf of a child for whom the taxpayer has already claimed an equivalent-to-spouse amount.

This credit, which applies for the full year, no matter which date the birth, adoption or death occurs during that year, is indexed for inflation.

## Infirm Dependant Credit

Where a relative over the age of 17 is dependent on the taxpayer by reason of mental or physical infirmity, the taxpayer may claim, as the federal portion of this credit, 15 per cent of $4,095, less the dependant's income in excess of $5,811, for a maximum credit of $614. The maximum available credit is eliminated entirely when the dependant's income reaches $9,906.

The corresponding provincial/territorial portion of this credit is as follows:

**Alberta:** The Alberta provincial portion of this credit is 10 per cent of up to $9,355, less the dependant's income in excess of $6,180, for a maximum credit of $936. The maximum available credit is eliminated entirely when the dependant's income reaches $15,535.

**British Columbia:** The British Columbia provincial portion of this credit is 5.06 per cent of up to $4,021, less the dependant's income in excess of $6,405, for a maximum credit of $203. The maximum available credit is eliminated entirely when the dependant's income reaches $10,426.

**Manitoba:** The Manitoba provincial portion of this credit is 10.90 per cent of up to $3,605, less the dependant's income in excess of $5,115, for a maximum credit of $393. The maximum available credit is eliminated entirely when the dependant's income reaches $8,720.

**New Brunswick:** The New Brunswick provincial portion of this credit is 10.12 per cent of up to $3,965, less the dependant's income in excess of $5,625, for a maximum credit of $401. The maximum available credit is eliminated entirely when the dependant's income reaches $9,590.

**Newfoundland and Labrador:** The Newfoundland and Labrador provincial portion of this credit in 2008 is an average of 8.20 per cent of up to $2,402, less the dependant's income in excess of an average amount of $5,164, for a maximum credit of $197. The maximum available credit is eliminated entirely when the dependant's income reaches $7,566.

**Northwest Territories:** The Northwest Territories territorial portion of this credit is 5.90 per cent of up to $4,095, less the dependant's income in excess of $5,811, for a maximum credit of $242. The maximum available credit is eliminated entirely when the dependant's income reaches $9,906.

**Nova Scotia:** The Nova Scotia provincial portion of this credit is 8.79 per cent of up to $2,551, less the dependant's income in excess of $5,180, for a maximum credit of $224. The maximum available credit is eliminated entirely when the dependant's income reaches $7,731.

**Nunavut:** The Nunavut territorial portion of this credit is 4 per cent of up to $4,095, less the dependant's income in excess of $5,811, for a maximum credit of $164. The maximum available credit is eliminated entirely when the dependant's income reaches $9,906.

**Ontario:** The Ontario provincial portion of this credit is 6.05 per cent of up to $4,091, less the dependant's income in excess of $5,817, for a maximum credit of $248. The maximum available credit is eliminated entirely when the dependant's income reaches $9,908.

**Prince Edward Island:** The Prince Edward Island provincial portion of this credit is 9.80 per cent of up to $2,446, less the dependant's income in excess of $4,966, for a maximum credit of $240. The maximum available credit is eliminated entirely when the dependant's income reaches $7,412.

**Quebec:** Applicable only to non-students at a rate of 20 per cent of $2,740, or $548, less 80 per cent of the dependant's net income (excluding scholarships, bursaries or awards), which eliminates the available credit at $3,425. However, this credit is not restricted to dependants by reason of mental or physical infirmity. It applies more broadly to a dependant over the age of 18, so long as the taxpayer has not claimed a transferred amount for a child over 18 enrolled in post-secondary studies.

**Saskatchewan:** The Saskatchewan provincial portion of this credit is 11 per cent of up to $8,190, less the dependant's income in excess of $5,811, for a maximum credit of $901. The maximum available credit is eliminated entirely when the dependant's income reaches $14,001.

**Yukon:** The Yukon territorial portion of this credit is 7.04 per cent of up to $4,095, less the dependant's income in excess of $5,811, for a maximum credit of $288. The maximum available credit is eliminated entirely when the dependant's income reaches $9,906.

To qualify, individuals must have supported the relative at some time during the year. The relative must be either a child or grandchild of the taxpayer or their spouse/common-law partner; or if residing in Canada at any time throughout the year, could also be the taxpayer's or their spouse/common-law partner's parent, grandparent, brother, sister, uncle, aunt, niece or nephew.

---

**Tax Tips**

You may be able to claim a dependant credit (or the equivalent-to-spouse credit) for a person by reason of their infirmity even if they do not qualify for the disability credit. The CRA considers a person to be infirm if they are dependent on the services of another individual for a considerable period of time.

---

## Caregiver Tax Credit

The caregiver tax credit reduces federal tax by up to $614 (15 per cent of $4,095) for individuals 18 years of age and over who are responsible for the in-home care of an infirm, dependent relative or parent/grandparent (including in-laws) who are at least 65 years of age. The maximum available credit is reduced by the dependant's net income in excess of $13,986 and eliminated entirely when their income reaches $18,081.

The corresponding provincial credits are as follows:

**Alberta:** The Alberta provincial tax credit involves a maximum of $936 (10 per cent of $9,355), which is reduced by 10 per cent of net income in excess of $14,874 and eliminated entirely when their income reaches $24,229.

**British Columbia:** The British Columbia provincial tax credit involves a maximum of $203 (5.06 per cent of $4,021), which is reduced by 5.06 per cent of net income in excess of $13,608 and eliminated entirely when their income reaches $17,629.

**Manitoba:** The Manitoba provincial tax credit involves a maximum of $393 (10.90 per cent of $3,605), which is reduced by 10.90 per cent of net income in excess of $12,312 and eliminated entirely when their income reaches $15,917.

**New Brunswick:** The New Brunswick provincial tax credit involves a maximum of $401 (10.12 per cent of $3,965), which is reduced by 10.12 per cent of net income in excess of $13,540 and eliminated entirely when their income reaches $17,505.

**Newfoundland and Labrador:** The Newfoundland and Labrador provincial tax credit in 2008 involves a maximum of $197 (based on an average of 8.20 per cent of $2,402), which is reduced by 8.20 per cent of net income in excess of an average amount of $11,743 and eliminated entirely when their income reaches $14,145.

**Northwest Territories:** The Northwest Territories territorial tax credit involves a maximum of $242 (5.90 per cent of $4,095), which is reduced by 5.90 per cent of net income in excess of $13,986 and eliminated entirely when their income reaches $18,081.

**Nova Scotia:** The Nova Scotia provincial tax credit involves a maximum of $392 (8.79 per cent of $4,465), which is reduced by 8.79 per cent of net income in excess of $12,467 and eliminated entirely when their income reaches $16,932.

**Nunavut:** The Nunavut territorial tax credit involves a maximum of $164 (4 per cent of $4,095), which is reduced by 4 per cent of net income in excess of $13,986 and eliminated entirely when their income reaches $18,081.

**Ontario:** The Ontario provincial tax credit involves a maximum of $248 (6.05 per cent of $4,092), which is reduced by 6.05 per cent of net income in excess of $13,999 and eliminated entirely when their income reaches $18,091.

**Prince Edward Island:** The Prince Edward Island provincial tax credit involves a maximum of $240 (9.8 per cent of $2,446), which is reduced by 9.8 per cent of net income in excess of $11,953 and eliminated entirely when their income reaches $14,399.

**Quebec:** Quebec has two refundable caregiver tax credits. One provides a credit of up to $1,033 in 2008 for the care of an eligible relative, reduced by 16 per cent of that relative's income in excess of $20,650.

A second refundable caregiver tax credit was introduced in 2008. It provides up to 30 per cent on $5,200 for a maximum credit of $1,560 for care provided to any eligible person, not just a relative. This credit is reduced by 3 per cent of the caregiver's family income in excess of $50,000.

**Saskatchewan:** The Saskatchewan provincial tax credit involves a maximum of $901 (11 per cent of $8,190), which is reduced by 11 per cent of net income in excess of $13,986 and eliminated entirely when their income reaches $22,176.

**Yukon:** The Yukon territorial tax credit involves a maximum of $288 (7.04 per cent of $4,095), which is reduced by 7.04 per cent of net income in excess of $13,986 and eliminated entirely when their income reaches $18,081.

Eligibility for this credit (as well as for the disability tax credit and supplement, and infirm-dependant credits) includes spouses or common-law partners of individuals who are dependent because of mental or physical infirmity; support may also be provided by certain caregivers living apart from their dependent relatives.

This credit is not available on behalf of an individual for whom the equivalent-to-spouse credit or infirm dependant credit has already been claimed.

## Tax Tips

If you take time off work to care for a gravely ill or dying family member, including a parent, spouse or child, you are eligible to be provided with employment insurance (EI) benefits for up to six weeks.

## Adoption Tax Credit

The 2005 federal budget introduced an adoption tax credit to cover up to $10,000 worth of eligible adoption expenses for a child of the taxpayer, including non-reimbursed items such as fees paid to an adoption agency that is licensed in a province or territory; court costs, legal and administrative expenses; and reasonable travel and living expenses required to secure an adoption, among others.

With indexing, the federal amount is $10,643 in 2008, for a credit of $1,596.

Six provinces and one territory have followed suit with similar legislation, and offer taxpayers in the following jurisdictions the following amounts and credits in 2008.

**Alberta** — Alberta has a provincial adoption tax credit in the amount of $11,053 (indexed), at a rate of 10 per cent, for a credit of $1,105.

**British Columbia** — British Columbia has a provincial adoption tax credit in the amount of $10,643 (indexed), at a rate of 5.06 per cent, for a credit of $539.

**Manitoba** — Manitoba has a provincial adoption tax credit in the amount of $10,000 (non-indexed), at a rate of 10.90 per cent, for a credit of $1,090.

**Newfoundland and Labrador** — Newfoundland and Labrador has a provincial adoption tax credit in the amount of $10,211 (indexed), at, for 2008, an average rate of 8.20 per cent, for a credit of $837.

**Ontario** — Ontario has a provincial adoption tax credit in the amount of $10,592 (indexed), at a rate of 6.05 per cent, for a credit of $641.

**Quebec** — Quebec has a refundable provincial adoption tax credit in the amount of $20,000 at a rate of 50 per cent, for a credit of $10,000.

**Yukon** — The Yukon Territory has a territorial adoption tax credit in the amount of $10,643 (indexed), at a rate of 7.04 per cent, for a credit of $749.

## Medical Expense Credit

An individual may claim a credit for any non-reimbursed medical expenses. The federal portion of this credit for the 2008 taxation year consists of 15 per cent of expenses in excess of the lesser of: $1,962; or 3 per cent of the individual's net income for the year. Such expenses may be incurred on the taxpayer's own behalf or that of their spouse or common-law partner, or child of the taxpayer under the age of 18.

Medical and disability related expenses may also be claimed by caregivers who are looking after an adult child 18 or over or somebody other than a spouse or common-law partner or dependant child; the amount they can claim is the lesser of: $10,000; or the amount by which expenses paid exceed $1,962; or 3 per cent of net income.

Provincially and in the Territories:

**Alberta:** The Alberta provincial portion of the medical expense credit consists of 10 per cent of expenses in excess of the lesser of: $2,088 or 3 per cent of the individual's net income for the year.

**British Columbia:** The British Columbia provincial portion of the medical expense credit consists of 5.06 per cent of expenses in excess of the lesser of: $1,911 or 3 per cent of the individual's net income for the year.

**Manitoba:** The Manitoba provincial portion of the medical expense credit consists of 10.90 per cent of expenses in excess of the lesser of: $1,728 or 3 per cent of the individual's net income for the year.

**New Brunswick:** The New Brunswick provincial portion of the medical expense credit consists of 10.12 per cent of expenses in excess of the lesser of: $1,899 or 3 per cent of the individual's net income for the year.

**Newfoundland and Labrador:** The Newfoundland and Labrador provincial portion of the medical expense credit in 2008 consists of an average rate of 8.20 per cent of expenses in excess of the lesser of an average amount, for 2008, of: $1,646 or 3 per cent of the individual's net income for the year.

**Northwest Territories:** The Northwest Territories territorial portion of the medical expense credit consists of 5.90 per cent of expenses in excess of the lesser of: $1,962 or 3 per cent of the individual's net income for the year.

**Nova Scotia:** The Nova Scotia provincial portion of the medical expense credit consists of 8.79 per cent of expenses in excess of the lesser of: $1,637 or 3 per cent of the individual's net income for the year.

**Nunavut:** The Nunavut territorial portion of the medical expense credit consists of 4 per cent of expenses in excess of the lesser of: $1,962 or 3 per cent of the individual's net income for the year.

**Ontario:** The Ontario provincial portion of the medical expense credit consists of 6.05 per cent of expenses in excess of the lesser of: $1,965 or 3 per cent of the individual's net income for the year.

**Prince Edward Island:** The Prince Edward Island provincial portion of the medical expense credit consists of 9.80 per cent of expenses in excess of the lesser of: $1,678 or 3 per cent of the individual's net income for the year.

**Quebec:** The Quebec provincial portion of the medical expense credit consists of 20.00 per cent of expenses in excess of 3 per cent of the taxpayer's family income for the year.

**Saskatchewan:** The Saskatchewan provincial portion of the medical expense credit consists of 11 per cent of expenses in excess of the lesser of: $1,962 or 3 per cent of the individual's net income for the year.

**Yukon:** The Yukon territorial portion of the medical expense credit consists of 7.04 per cent of expenses in excess of the lesser of: $1,962 or 3 per cent of the individual's net income for the year.

In each province or territory, when medical expenses are claimed for dependants other than a spouse or common-law partner, the total expenses claimed might need to be reduced by a certain percentage of that dependant's income in excess of the provincial or territorial portion of the basic credit. Check with your Certified General Accountant for details.

Generally, medication must be prescribed by a registered physician or dentist, and dispensed and recorded by a qualified pharmacist if such expenses are eligible to be claimed for the medical expense tax credit. Payments may also be issued indirectly to a medical practitioner — i.e., through an institution that provides medical services on their behalf.

Receipts must support expenses claimed. Normally, these expenses can be claimed for any 12-month period ending in the year, but should the return be prepared for a deceased taxpayer, that period is expanded to encompass claims for any 24-month period, including the individual's date of death.

## Eligible Medical Expenses

The list of expenses eligible for the federal medical expense tax credit includes, but is certainly not limited to:

- attendant care for workers with disabilities — up to two-thirds of earned income with no maximum;
- full-time attendant care for individuals with severe and prolonged mental or physical impairments, including all expenses with no maximum;
- supervision of an individual eligible for the disability tax credit who is residing in a Canadian group home devoted to the care of people with a severe and prolonged impairment;
- part-time attendant care — up to $10,000, increasing to $20,000 if the individual died during the year;
- a block, or annual fee, paid to a medical centre or physician to cover uninsured medical services;

- 50 per cent of the cost of an air conditioner needed for a severe chronic ailment, to a maximum of $1,000;
- 20 per cent of the cost of a van that is, or will be, adapted for the transportation of an individual using a wheelchair, to a maximum of $5,000;
- expenses incurred for moving to accessible housing, to a maximum of $2,000;
- a device such as a wheelchair to assist an individual with a mobility problem;
- sign language interpreter fees;
- voice recognition software necessary to assist a person with a disability;
- various medical devices, along with accessories, required to assist with impaired seeing or hearing;
- tutoring services from a non-related person for individuals with a certified learning disability or mental impairment;
- certain costs related to attending an educational facility with specialized personnel, equipment or facilities to address a physical or mental impairment;
- a portion of reasonable expenses relating to construction or renovation costs incurred to assist an individual with a severe disability gain access to, or be mobile or functional within their principal place of residence;
- reasonable expenses for driveway alterations made to enable a mobility-impaired individual to access a bus; and
- reasonable travel expenses incurred to obtain medical services not available in the vicinity of the patient's home, to the extent these have not been reimbursed by a provincial/territorial health plan, or other source. See also Travel Expense Claims, page 88.

The list of expenses eligible for the medical expense credit is lengthy. For a review of eligible medical expenses, refer to CRA publication IT519R2 or other related documents. Also check with your province or territory to see if additional expenses and/or indexing may apply.

## Tax Tips

A pharmacist is also considered to be a medical practitioner. Therefore, if your pharmacist provides such services as running a disease management clinic or other activities for which a fee is payable, this may qualify as a deductible medical expense.

## Other Medical Credits

A refundable tax credit of up to $500 is available to individuals with high medical expenses and low annual income. There are also broad rules governing income earned by a trust established for the benefit of a person with a disability, and duty-free goods for individuals that have disabilities.

Some taxpayers may also qualify for a federal refundable medical expense supplement of up to $1,041 (up from $1,022 in 2007). The actual supplement amount is the lesser of: $1,041 or 25 per cent of attendant care expenses claimed under the disability supports deduction (see below), plus 25 per cent of allowable expenses claimed under the medical expense tax credit.

To qualify for this supplement, taxpayers must be 18 years of age or older and have total business and employment income of at least $3,040 for the year. This supplement is reduced by 5 per cent of family net income in excess of $23,057.

## Disability Supports Deduction

The 2004 federal budget introduced a new disability supports deduction. It includes attendant care expenses, plus other disability support expenses that have not otherwise been reimbursed and have been incurred to enable an eligible individual to work, attend secondary school or a designated educational institution. Under this provision the maximum deduction is the lesser of: eligible non-reimbursed expenses and earned income for the year. If attending school, it is the lesser of: eligible non-reimbursed expenses and the least of three amounts — the amount by which total income exceeds earned income; $15,000; and $375 times the number of weeks they are in attendance at that school.

Expenses claimed under the disability supports deduction, which include various devices and services to deal with vision, hearing, speaking and mobility restrictions, among others, cannot also be claimed under the medical expense tax credit.

## Other Points Related to Disability and Medical Expenses

Use of the disability tax credit on the tax return of a deceased individual may still be applicable in the year of death if a medical doctor certified before death that the individual had a "severe and prolonged mental or physical impairment" which was reasonably expected to last for at least 12 months.

For 2002 and subsequent taxation years, seniors that are living in a retirement home and who also qualify for the DTC may claim attendant care expenses of up to $10,000 per year (their estate may claim $20,000 for the year of death).

The attendant care component of fees paid to a retirement home includes the salary and wages paid to employees with respect to the following services provided to a senior:

- health care;
- meal preparation;
- housekeeping in the resident's personal living space;
- laundry for the resident's personal items;

- a transportation driver; and
- security, where applicable.

The retirement home must provide the taxpayer or their caregivers with a receipt showing the applicable amounts paid for attendant care. Eligible seniors who wish to request an adjustment for the 2002 taxation year may do so either through a letter to the CRA that includes the senior's social insurance number (SIN), address, daytime phone number and supporting documentation or by completing Form T1-ADJ — *T1 Adjustment Request* (online at www.cra-arc.gc.ca/E/pbg/tf/t1-adj/README.html).

The attendant care change may also apply to taxation years prior to 2002 if a Notice of Objection ruling is still outstanding or can still be filed.

Generally, expenses paid to a nursing home qualify as tax-deductible medical expenses while those paid to a personal care institution do not, because the care provided to patients in a nursing home tends to be more extensive. However, there may be exceptions to that rule. All or part of the remuneration paid to a personal care facility might, for instance, be deductible in situations where an individual with a severe and prolonged impairment requires specialized equipment, facilities or personnel.

Caregivers are also able to deduct reasonable expenses associated with the cost of training required to care for dependant relatives with mental or physical infirmities.

Patients who are incapable of travelling without the assistance of an attendant may be able to deduct a full range of reasonable travel expenses on behalf of somebody required to assist them to travel to a facility at least 80 kilometres away from home to seek proper medical treatment.

Certain expenses incurred for the purpose of providing care to a person with a disability are exempt from the goods and services tax (GST) and harmonized sales tax (HST). These include a government funded homemaker service provided to an individual in their place of residence, various medical devices and some recreational programs. For a complete list, consult CRA's guide RC4064, *Information Concerning People with Disabilities.*

## Tuition Fee and Education Credits

Post-secondary students who are not otherwise reimbursed for the cost of their courses, or who have received financial assistance such as a grant, benefit or other allowance, are generally entitled to a credit for the cost of the courses and certain related school fees that they or their families must pay.

In order to qualify, full-time students must generally be taking courses of at least three consecutive weeks involving at least 10 hours of study per week for the duration of the course at a designated educational institution. Typically this is at a university, college or other school in Canada that offers courses at a post-secondary level, or internationally at a university or in a university-related course that leads to a degree.

In 2008, these students may claim a federal credit of 15 per cent of eligible tuition fees, plus an education credit of 15 per cent of $400 per month, or $60, with the education credit allowable only if they are attending a designated educational institution as defined by the federal government.

Provincially and territorially, taxpayers may also claim the tuition fee credit, based on a percentage of eligible tuition fees (except for Quebec). They may also deduct for the education tax credit as follows:

**Alberta:** In Alberta, this credit is indexed; students may claim a monthly provincial credit of up to 10 per cent of $628, or $63.

**British Columbia:** In British Columbia, students may claim a monthly provincial credit of up to 5.06 per cent of $200, or $10.

**Manitoba:** In Manitoba, students may claim a monthly provincial credit of up to 10.90 per cent of $400, or $44.

**New Brunswick:** In New Brunswick, students may claim a monthly provincial credit of up to 10.12 per cent of $400, or $40.

**Newfoundland and Labrador:** In Newfoundland and Labrador, students may claim a monthly provincial credit in 2008 averaging 8.20 per cent of $200, or $16.

**Northwest Territories:** In the Northwest Territories, students may claim a monthly territorial credit of up to 5.90 per cent of $400, or $24.

**Nova Scotia:** In Nova Scotia, students may claim a monthly provincial credit of up to 8.79 per cent of $200, or $18.

**Nunavut:** In Nunavut, students may claim a monthly territorial credit of up to 4 per cent of $400, or $16.

**Ontario:** In Ontario, this credit is indexed; students may claim a monthly provincial credit of up to 6.05 per cent of $468, or $28.

**Prince Edward Island:** In Prince Edward Island, students may claim a monthly provincial credit of up to 9.80 per cent of $400, or $39.

**Quebec:** See explanation in Appendix I.

**Saskatchewan:** In Saskatchewan, students may claim a monthly provincial credit of up to 11 per cent of $400, or $44.

**Yukon:** In the Yukon, students may claim a monthly territorial credit of up to 7.04 per cent of $400, or $28.

To qualify for these credits, students need not be in full-time attendance, but only enrolled as full-time students. Students with disabilities may also be enrolled part-time to qualify for a full-time credit.

Students who are engaged in part-time studies — defined as a minimum of three consecutive weeks involving at least 12 hours of course work a month at a designated educational institution in Canada only (although exceptions might apply for part-time students who live in Canada and commute to a listed school in the U.S.) — may also claim the federal tuition fee credit of 15 per cent of eligible tuition fees, plus a provincial or territorial credit at applicable rates. In 2008, they may also deduct $120 a month, or $18 toward eligibility for the 15 per cent federal education tax credit.

Provincially and territorially, the corresponding part-time education credit amounts are:

**Alberta:** In Alberta, this credit is indexed; students may claim a monthly provincial credit of up to 10 per cent of $188, or $19.

**British Columbia:** In British Columbia, students may claim a monthly provincial credit of up to 5.06 per cent of $60, or $3.

**Manitoba:** In Manitoba, students may claim a monthly provincial credit of up to 10.90 per cent of $120, or $13.

**New Brunswick:** In New Brunswick, students may claim a monthly provincial credit of up to 10.12 per cent of $120, or $12.

**Newfoundland and Labrador:** In Newfoundland and Labrador, students may claim an average monthly provincial credit in 2008 of up to 8.20 per cent of $60, or $5.

**Northwest Territories:** In the Northwest Territories, students may claim a monthly territorial credit of up to 5.90 per cent of $120, or $7.

**Nova Scotia:** In Nova Scotia, students may claim a monthly provincial credit of up to 8.79 per cent of $60, or $5.

**Nunavut:** In Nunavut, students may claim a monthly territorial credit of up to 4 per cent of $120, or $5.

**Ontario:** In Ontario, this credit is indexed; students may claim a monthly provincial credit of up to 6.05 per cent of $140, or $8.

**Prince Edward Island:** In Prince Edward Island, students may claim a monthly provincial credit of up to 9.80 per cent of $120, or $12.

**Quebec:** See explanation in Appendix I.

**Saskatchewan:** In Saskatchewan, students may claim a monthly provincial credit of up to 11 per cent of $120, or $13.

**Yukon:** In the Yukon, students may claim a monthly territorial credit of up to 7.04 per cent of $120, or $8.

The same transfer and carryforward provisions applicable to full-time students also apply to part-time students.

## Additional Points Relating to Tuition Fee and Education Tax Credits

People with disabilities who are enrolled in Human Resources and Skills Development Canada (HRSDC) or equivalent provincial/territorial-approved training programs can deduct those related expenses. Under this adult basic education (ABE) deduction, such courses may, for instance, allow taxpayers to finish high school, improve their literacy skills or upgrade existing educational credentials in order to improve their employment chances. (Note: The ABE deduction is retroactive and might apply to financial assistance received during taxation years after 1996 and before this announcement in 2001.)

The 2004 federal budget expanded provisions of the education tax credit to include students who are pursuing career-related post-secondary education at their own expense. Note, however, that courses taken outside of a university that are designed to improve personal skills would not likely qualify for the tuition tax credit. The *Income Tax Act* states that, to qualify for this credit, such courses must be designed to improve occupational skills and be held at a certified place of instruction.

Students who are enrolled in two designated educational institutions in order to achieve a combined course load equivalent to that of a full-time student may be entitled to the full-time education tax credit, provided at least one of the designated institutions issues the appropriate T2202 or T2202A form if a Canadian institution, or TL11A, TL11C or TL11D form if outside the country, to indicate that the courses taken at both schools qualify them for that status.

There are some mandatory ancillary charges, such as fees for computer services, labs, health and athletics, which are also eligible for the tuition credit. Tuition fees at a qualified Canadian educational facility must exceed $100 per institution (this requirement is waived for foreign universities provided the full-time student is attending a course of at least 13 weeks' duration leading to a degree) and be claimed on a calendar-year basis. Courses must be taken at a post-secondary level or be for occupational skills provided by a qualified educational institution for students 16 or older.

The 2006 federal budget introduced a textbook tax credit for students eligible for the full-time and part-time education tax credits. In 2008, the federal textbook credit is 15 per cent of $65, or $10 per month for full-time students, and 15 per cent of $20, or $3 for part-time students.

Nunavut has matched this federal provision, and in 2008, their territorial textbook tax credit is 4 per cent of $65, or $3, and the part-time textbook credit is 4 per cent of $20, or $1, per month.

The Yukon Territory has also matched this federal provision, and in 2008, their territorial textbook tax credit is 7.04 per cent of $65, or $5, and the part-time textbook credit is 7.04 per cent of $20, or $1, per month.

The 2006 budget also fully exempted all scholarship, fellowship or bursary income with respect to post-secondary education or occupational training from taxation, provided it applies to enrolment in a program that entitles the student to claim the education tax credit. Previously, only the first $3,000 of such income was exempt.

Taxpayers who are receiving financial assistance for their post-secondary education through the EI or a similar provincial program also have access to the education tax credit.

Furthermore, students need not necessarily be in physical attendance at a qualified institution in Canada to claim either the tuition or education tax credits. Recent court rulings have interpreted the *Income Tax Act* differently with respect to whether students must physically attend a designated institution outside Canada in order to claim the tuition tax credit. However, there now appears to be a general acceptance that they do not. Therefore, online course participation through, for example, the Internet website of a recognized post-secondary institution either in Canada or internationally may also qualify the taxpayer for both tax credits.

## Transfer of Credits

Unused tuition, education and textbook credits may be carried forward indefinitely to offset the student's income taxes in future years. Alternatively, students may transfer unused federal credits of up to $5,000, and the same amount provincially/territorially (Ontario's rate is indexed to $6,003), reduced by their income in excess of personal credits, to a supporting person, such as a parent or grandparent, but the transferred credits must be claimed in the year incurred.

Students who are attending an accredited institution outside Canada — generally in a university level course of at least 13 consecutive weeks duration leading to a degree — are eligible to transfer their unused credits provided they owe Canadian income tax. All, or at least a substantial portion of their income, must be considered taxable income earned in Canada during the year the tuition fees were incurred.

Consult your Certified General Accountant if you attend a higher education facility outside Canada.

## Student Loan Interest Tax Credit

A 15 per cent federal tax credit and a provincial/territorial tax credit are available on the repayment of interest on federally or provincially approved student loans. The provincial and territorial tax credit corresponds to the rate in the lowest tax bracket for that jurisdiction (see Appendix III, page 201).

To be eligible, however, students must consolidate their loans with an authorized lender after graduating, and assume responsibility for paying interest by the first day of the seventh month following completion of their studies.

Students have the option of applying that non-transferable credit to either the current year or up to five subsequent taxation years.

## Pension Income Credit

The federal government allows a 15 per cent federal tax credit on up to $2,000 of eligible pension income (non-indexed). In 2008, this amounts to a maximum of $300.

Provincial/territorial tax credits at the lowest taxation rates in each jurisdiction are also available on up to $1,000 of eligible pension income (with the exception of Nunavut and the Yukon Territory, which mirror the federal government at $2,000 for a territorial credit of $80 in Nunavut and $141 in Yukon, and Quebec, which offers up to $1,500, for a credit of $300). In Alberta, Nova Scotia and Ontario this pension is indexed from a base of $1,000; it stands at $1,244 in Alberta (for a credit of $124), $1,069 in Nova Scotia (for a credit of $94), and $1,201 in Ontario (for a credit of $73) for the 2008 taxation year.

The rest of the provinces and territories provide a credit on $1,000 at their applicable provincial rates. These are included in Appendix I on page 179.

Taxpayers may also transfer to their return any unused pension income credit belonging to their spouse or common-law partner.

Eligible pension income includes:

- life annuity receipts from a superannuation or pension fund, regardless of the recipient's age;
- annuity receipts under an RRSP or DPSP, amounts received from an RRIF and certain other non-government annuities, provided the recipient is at least 65 by the end of the year, or the amounts are received as a consequence of a spouse/common-law partner's death; or

- foreign source pensions, such as United States social security and United Kingdom pension income, to the extent such income cannot be excluded as a result of an existing tax convention between Canada and a foreign country.

Payments to an LRIF, or similar locked-in tax instrument, which are treated like RRSPs and RRIFs for tax purposes, may also qualify for a pension income deduction.

Ineligible pension income includes:

- Canada Pension Plan (CPP), Quebec Pension Plan (QPP) and Old Age Security (OAS);
- lump-sum payments from a pension or superannuation plan;
- death benefits;
- retiring allowances;
- amounts received under a salary deferral arrangement;
- payments received out of a retirement compensation arrangement; or
- any other qualifying income that has been rolled over to an RPP or an RRSP.

Beginning in 2007, the federal government allows taxpayers to split pension income with their spouse or common-law partner, by allocating up to one-half of their qualified income. When pension income has been allocated in such fashion, both partners must make a joint election on Form T1032 — *Joint Election to Split Pension Income*. Many provinces and territories have followed suit with parallel measures.

Amounts transferred to spouses under the age of 65 might not be eligible for the pension deduction.

## Tax Tips

If you are 65, consider creating pension income by converting part of your RRSP to a life annuity or an RRIF if your financial circumstances warrant such a move.

Contributing to a spousal RRSP also creates potential pension income for your spouse or common-law partner.

## Charitable Donation Credit

The federal charitable donation tax credit is calculated as 15 per cent on the first $200 of eligible donations, plus 29 per cent of any amount in excess of $200.

The corresponding provincial tax is as follows:

**Alberta:** For Alberta residents, it is 10 per cent of the first $200 and 21 per cent for any amount over $200.

**British Columbia:** For British Columbia residents, it is 5.06 per cent of the first $200 and 14.70 per cent for any amount over $200.

**Manitoba:** For Manitoba residents, it is 10.90 per cent of the first $200 and 17.40 per cent for any amount over $200.

**New Brunswick:** For New Brunswick residents, it is 10.12 per cent of the first $200 and 17.95 per cent for any amount over $200.

**Newfoundland and Labrador:** For Newfoundland and Labrador residents, for 2008 it is an average of 8.20 per cent of the first $200 and an average of 16 per cent for any amount over $200.

**Northwest Territories:** For Northwest Territories residents, it is 5.90 per cent of the first $200 and 14.05 per cent for any amount over $200.

**Nova Scotia:** For Nova Scotia residents, it is 8.79 per cent of the first $200 and 17.50 per cent of any amount over $200.

**Nunavut:** For Nunavut residents, it is 4 per cent of the first $200 and 11.50 per cent for any amount over $200.

**Ontario:** For Ontario residents, it is 6.05 per cent of the first $200 and 11.16 per cent for any amount over $200.

**Prince Edward Island:** For Prince Edward Island residents, it is 9.80 per cent of the first $200 and 16.70 per cent for any amount over $200.

**Quebec:** For Quebec residents, it is 20 per cent of the first $200 and 24 per cent for any amount over $200.

**Saskatchewan:** For Saskatchewan residents, it is 11 per cent of the first $200 and 15.00 per cent for any amount over $200.

**Yukon:** For Yukon residents, it is 7.04 per cent of the first $200 and 12.76 per cent for any amount over $200.

A credit can be claimed for donations made in the current and/or the preceding five years (if not already claimed) based on an annual limit — generally 75 per cent of net income. That increases to 100 per cent in the taxpayer's year of death and for the preceding year.

## Other Points Related to Donations

Donations of appreciated capital property giving rise to capital gains also benefit from higher limits of up to 100 per cent of net income. Note, however, that the federal government introduced a rule, effective December 5, 2003, which limits the value of a gift of property for charitable donation purposes to the donor's cost of the property, where such property has been donated within three years of acquisition. Check with your Certified General Accountant for details.

Where a donation other than cash has been made to a registered charity, the charity must issue a receipt for the fair market value of the property at the time the gift was made.

A taxpayer may claim a credit with respect to charitable donations made outside Canada provided it is made to an organization that the federal government, or representatives thereof, have made a gift to during either the current year or the preceding 12 months.

The income inclusion rate on capital gains arising from donations of publicly traded securities made to recipients other than private foundations used to be 25 per cent. The 2006 federal budget entirely eliminated the income inclusion rate for such donations, effective May 2, 2006. It also eliminated any tax inclusion for qualifying charitable donations of listed publicly traded securities acquired with employee stock options, as well as in certain instances where taxpayers donate ecologically sensitive land, also effective May 2, 2006.

Special rules may also apply for donations of certain securities to private charitable foundations on or after March 19, 2007.

Consult your Certified General Accountant if you have questions about the proper tax treatment of charitable donations you make, particularly if these involve donations of property.

## Credit for Public Transit Pass

A federal non-refundable tax credit is available for taxpayers who purchase eligible weekly (involving at least four consecutive weekly passes per month), monthly or longer transit passes. In some instances, even shorter duration passes or electronic payment cards might be acceptable if they accumulate to allow for equivalent travel over a month or longer. Public transit could include transit of various modes, such as local bus, streetcar, subway, commuter train or bus, or local ferry. This credit applies at the rate of 15 per cent for 2008.

The Yukon Territory also introduced a tax credit for public transit passes in 2006; in 2008 this applies at the rate of 7.04 per cent.

This credit is transferable to a spouse or common-law partner, as well as to parents of dependent children under the age of 19.

### Tax Tips

Save applicable public transit passes in order to verify the expenses you are claiming for this tax credit.

If, during the course of your commute, you need to take your automobile on a ferry for which you pay monthly or longer fees, you may claim a public transit credit for the ferry costs relating directly to the transport of you and/or other family members, but not those for your automobile.

## Credit for Enrolment in Children's Fitness Programs

To encourage greater involvement in physical-fitness programs, the 2006 federal budget introduced a fitness tax credit of up to $500 against eligible fees paid for children under 16 who are enrolled in certain sports and physical-fitness program activities.

This credit, which took effect January 1, 2007, requires that "substantially all of the activities (undertaken) must include a significant amount of physical activity that contributes to cardio-respiratory endurance plus one or more of: muscular strength, muscular endurance, flexibility or balance."

The CRA lists several supervised children's programs as examples of recreational activities eligible for this tax credit, including hockey, skating, soccer, karate, football, basketball, folk dancing, swimming, hiking, horseback riding and sailing.

The programs must be ongoing, which is defined as being either a minimum of eight weeks' duration with at least one eligible physical activity session per week; or, if a children's camp, five consecutive days, provided more than 50 per cent of that time is devoted to physical activity.

The programs must be ongoing. For example, the prescribed programs of physical activity include: a weekly program involving a minimum of eight consecutive weeks' duration "in which all or substantially all of the activities include a significant amount of physical activity." They also include programs of at least five consecutive days, provided more than 50 per cent of that time is devoted to physical activity, such as a summer or day camp program. Similarly, membership in a club, association or other organization for eight consecutive weeks or longer may also qualify provided more than 50 per cent of the activities, or the time scheduled for such activities, are devoted to programs deemed eligible for this credit.

A pro-rated credit is available to cover membership and registration fees for programs in which 50 per cent or fewer of the activities are eligible.

For children that are eligible for the disability tax credit, the fitness tax credit applies if they are under the age of 18; plus there is a separate $500 credit, for a total of $1,000, available to them provided at least $100 is spent on registration fees for an eligible program.

The maximum taxable federal benefit is 15 per cent of $500, or $75. For taxpayers with children eligible for a $1,000 credit, the benefit doubles to $150.

Manitoba, Nova Scotia and the Yukon also provide a children's fitness tax credit on amounts up to $500, at provincial/territorial rates. Manitoba and the Yukon match the additional $500 provision, for a total of $1,000, for children that are eligible for the disability tax credit.

## Tax Tips

If you pay family membership fees in a program that involves eligible fitness activities, mixed with other activities, you might be able to apply a pro-rated portion to the children's fitness credit. Make sure you get a receipt from the organization clearly stating the amount that is eligible for a credit.

## Canada Pension Plan (CPP) and Employment Insurance (EI) Premiums Credit

Individuals who are paying Canada Pension Plan (CPP) and/or Employment Insurance (EI) premiums may claim a 15 per cent federal tax credit, as well as a provincial/territorial tax credit on the amount paid at the rate corresponding to the lowest tax bracket in their jurisdiction.

Self-employed individuals who are paying both the employee and employer portion of CPP premiums may claim a non-refundable credit for one-half the full 9.9 per cent contribution amount — in effect, the employee portion of the CPP (which amounts to 4.95 per cent) — and a deduction from income for the employer's half (also 4.95 per cent). However, self-employed taxpayers do not pay EI premiums related to self-employment income.

In 2008, the maximum federal tax credit available for CPP premiums paid is 15 per cent of $2,049, or $307. For EI premiums paid it is 15 per cent of $711, or $107.

See Appendix I on page 179 for the applicable provincial and territorial rates.

# OTHER TAX CREDITS

## Working Income Tax Benefit (WITB)

The 2007 federal budget introduced a refundable working income tax benefit (WITB) that provides up to $510 for individual taxpayers 19 or over without dependants, whose earned income exceeds $3,000, reduced by 15 per cent of net family income in excess of $9,681. The WITB is $1,019 for families, including couples or single parents 19 or over, with earned income in excess of $3,000, reduced by 15 per cent of net family income in excess of $14,776.

The WITB is calculated at the rate of 20 per cent of each dollar of earned income in excess of $3,000, therefore reaching a maximum benefit at $5,550 of earned income for individuals and $8,095 of earned income for families.

Individuals who are not classified as dependants; who are eligible for the disability tax credit (DTC); and have at least $1,750 in earned income will also receive an additional disability supplement that will provide up to a maximum credit of $255. This disability supplement is reduced by 15 per cent of net family income in excess of $13,077 for single individuals and $21,569 for families.

Full-time students with no dependants are not eligible for this WITB.

The amounts for both the WITB and WITB supplement vary for residents of British Columbia, Nunavut and Quebec.

## Goods and Services Tax (GST)

Canada's goods and services tax (GST) was reduced from 6 per cent to 5 per cent, effective January 1, 2008.

The harmonized sales tax (HST) rates applicable to New Brunswick, Nova Scotia and Newfoundland and Labrador, which combine GST and provincial tax, dropped from 14 per cent to 13 per cent, on January 1, 2008, in response to the latest change.

## Goods and Services Tax (GST) Credit

Beginning in July 2008, eligible individuals received a goods and services tax (GST) credit that increased to $242 per adult and $127 per qualified dependent child under age 19, subject to an income test based on family net income. A supplementary goods and services tax credit (GSTC) is also available for individuals with no spouse or common-law partner.

For taxpayers without dependants, this supplement is phased in at 2 per cent of net income in excess of $7,851, up to a maximum of $127, (with the total credit being reduced by 5 per cent of family net income in excess of $31,524). Single parents automatically receive the full $127 GST supplement, without any phase-in dependent on income.

The GST credit and supplement are fully indexed for inflation on an annual basis every July 1.

Only one spouse or common-law partner can claim the GST credit on behalf of both spouses and any dependants.

GST credits are paid separately, on a quarterly basis, in July, October, January and April. When the total credit is less than $100, only one annual payment is made, during July.

The GST credit responds to changes in family circumstances, such as the birth of a child, alteration in marital status or the taxpayer's attaining the age of 19, in the quarter following such an event. In order for the CRA to respond expeditiously to the taxpayer's personal changes, however, the relevant information must be relayed to the Agency on time.

HST administration is handled by the federal government and credit provisions related to the HST in New Brunswick, Nova Scotia and Newfoundland and Labrador are very similar to those of the GST.

## Tax Tips

You must file an income tax return in order to be eligible to receive the GST credit. Claim $242 (rather than $127) for a dependant claimed as "equivalent-to-spouse."

## Political Contribution Tax Credit

Contributions to a registered federal political party or a candidate in a federal election are eligible for a tax credit against federal income tax payable in the year the contribution was made, provided they are supported by valid receipts.

The federal tax credit calculation takes into account:

- three-quarters of the first $400; plus
- one-half of the next $350; and
- one-third of contributions between $750 and $1,275.

Thus, the maximum allowable tax credit of $650 is reached as a result of a political contribution totalling at least $1,275.

Similar provisions are also available for all provinces and territories, although each jurisdiction has a separate calculation for its respective tax credit.

## Tax Tips

To maximize the political contribution tax credit, consider spreading contributions over several years if you wish to donate more than the maximum allowable annual amount for tax purposes.

## Foreign Tax Credit

Canadian residents are taxable in Canada on world income from all sources. Income from foreign jurisdictions may also be subject to tax in that jurisdiction.

Foreign tax paid may be claimed as a foreign tax credit against Canadian taxes, subject to limitations. Foreign income that is exempt from tax in a foreign jurisdiction pursuant to say, a tax treaty, might not be included in the foreign income base for purposes of the tax credit calculation. Although this income may be exempt in a foreign jurisdiction, however, it must still be included in the taxpayer's world income for Canadian tax purposes.

The onus is on Canadian residents who receive income from foreign sources to ensure that any tax withheld from their pay pursuant to a tax treaty currently in effect between Canada and that country is withheld in the correct amount and percentage.

A separate credit calculation is required for both business and non-business income of each source country. Using Form T1135, taxpayers are also required to annually report specified foreign assets whose total cost exceeded $100,000 at any time during the previous taxation year.

Social security taxes paid to a foreign government are not eligible for Canadian foreign tax credits, with the exception of certain taxes paid in the U.S. covered by provisions in the Canada-United States Income Tax Convention.

## Overseas Employment Tax Credit (OETC)

A Canadian resident who performs substantially all employment duties outside of Canada in the course of a taxation year while an employee of a specified employer to whom he/she is at arm's length (also usually a resident of Canada), or sub-contractor thereof, may qualify for the overseas employment tax credit (OETC).

Specified employers must carry on business in the same country where employees, including professional, administrative and other support staff, perform their duties. Such jobs are generally held in connection with an overseas natural resource, construction, installation, agricultural or engineering project.

This credit potentially shelters from federal tax up to 80 per cent of their overseas employment income — including salary, wages and other remuneration like gratuities, taxable benefits and stock options — netted off by a reasonable proportion of allowable employment deductions, to a maximum of $100,000 (i.e., sheltering up to $80,000).

In 2008, provincial and territorial residents may deduct a certain percentage of the federal OETC, as follows:

| | |
|---|---|
| Alberta: | 35.00 per cent |
| British Columbia: | Expressed as a variable percentage of provincial tax divided by federal tax, with both figures being calculated before taking into account the OETC. |
| Manitoba: | 50.00 per cent |
| New Brunswick: | 57.00 per cent |

| | |
|---|---|
| Newfoundland and Labrador: | 54.70 per cent |
| Northwest Territories: | 45.00 per cent |
| Nova Scotia: | 57.50 per cent |
| Nunavut: | 45.00 per cent |
| Ontario: | 38.48 per cent |
| Prince Edward Island: | 57.50 per cent |
| Quebec: | An individual residing in Quebec who performs almost all of their duties pertaining to their employment outside Canada for a period of at least 30 consecutive days may take advantage of a deduction, in calculating their taxable income, of up to 100 per cent of basic salary and allowances of up to 50 per cent of basic salary. Not based on a percentage of the federal OETC. Special qualifying rules apply. |
| Saskatchewan: | 50.00 per cent |
| Yukon: | 44.00 per cent |

To qualify for the OETC, the CRA specifies that the taxpayer must work overseas for at least six consecutive months either in one calendar year, or overlapping the previous or next year; however, a 2002 court decision (Rooke) also ruled that, as long as the taxpayer performed all or substantially all of the work outside Canada over the course of a particular taxation year, he/she would be entitled to the deduction.

"All or substantially all" generally refers to at least 90 per cent of the employee's income being derived from eligible activities during the qualifying period for the OETC.

During this period the taxpayer can still take leave for vacation time and other activities, such as returning to Canada to meet with his/her employer and/or work briefly here, without prejudicing his/her status in terms of qualifying for the OETC — provided he/she continues to perform a substantial amount of his/her employment duties outside Canada.

An individual who would otherwise be employed by a foreign company but instead incorporates a Canadian company, which in turn contracts with the foreign company to provide services, cannot claim this amount.

This credit is also disallowed if the Canadian company does not employ more than five full-time employees and the taxpayer is a specified shareholder, or is related to a specified shareholder, who owns at least 10 per cent of the shares together with non-arm's-length parties of the business.

An amendment to this provision of the *Income Tax Act* has been proposed whereby at least 10 per cent of the qualified employer's shares, or the value of any partnership interests, must be held by persons resident in Canada.

The CRA recognizes the Government of Canada as a specified employer. Therefore, federal government employees might qualify for the OETC if employed overseas as the result of a government contract, although services provided under a prescribed international development assistance program by the federal government are excluded.

Income used by the taxpayer to calculate the OETC may not be used in the calculation of the foreign tax credit.

## Tax Tips

Activities performed under contract with the United Nations might qualify taxpayers for an OETC credit.

## Scientific Research and Experimental Development Tax Credit (SR&ED)

Generous tax incentives exist to encourage investment in research and development (R&D) activities. A scientific research and experimental development investment tax credit (SR&ED ITC) is, for instance, available on qualified capital and current expenditures. This SR&ED ITC can reduce tax payable and/or result in a cash refund.

Canadian-controlled private corporations may be eligible for SR&ED ITCs at a rate of 35 per cent on the first $2 million of annual eligible expenditures (the 2008 budget proposes to increase this limit to $3 million for taxation years that end on or after February 26, 2008) and 20 per cent thereafter (although the $3 million expenditure limit might be reduced as taxable income for the previous taxation year rises above $400,000 in 2008, and as taxable capital of the previous year exceeds $10 million). Other Canadian companies, along with individuals, are eligible for SR&ED ITCs at a rate of 20 per cent. SR&ED ITC eligible activities must be business-related and carried on in Canada; this could also include areas considered part of the country's exclusive economic zone, including its airspace, seabed or subsoil.

The 2008 budget also proposes to increase the upper limit of the phase-out range from income of $600,000 to $700,000; and of taxable capital from $15 million to $50 million for taxation years that end on or after February 26, 2008.

Investment tax credits can be carried back up to 3 years, and, as announced in the 2006 federal budget, forward up to 20 years (double the previous 10-year entitlement) for losses incurred and credits earned in taxation years ending after 2005. The federal government has proposed expanding this provision to cover losses and credits pertaining to the taxation years 1998 to 2005, inclusive.

Several provincial and at least one territorial jurisdiction (the Yukon) offer R&D tax credit programs related to the SR&ED ITC credit.

Check with your Certified General Accountant to see if and how this credit might apply to certain activities and expenditures related to your business.

## Tax Tips

Carefully monitor the use of related materials that comprise a portion of your SR&ED ITC. Such costs are only permitted in the ITC calculation to the extent they are actually applied in the research and development process, as opposed to some other commercial use.

You need not have incurred the SR&ED expenditures during the year in which a related deduction is claimed.

Because the opportunity for a SR&ED ITC will generally be lost if the claim is not filed on time, it is a good idea for businesses or individuals that wish to make a claim to do so well in advance of the final due date. It is best to provide the CRA with enough time to review the claims and confirm that everything required has been received.

# ADDITIONAL TAX CONSIDERATIONS

## Canada Child Tax Benefit

The Canada Child Tax Benefit (CCTB) is an income-tested benefit with two components: the CCTB base benefit for low and middle-income families and the National Child Benefit (NCB) supplement for low-income families. It involves a monthly non-taxable payment made to a custodial parent of children under the age of 18.

The CCTB and NCB supplement are both fully indexed for inflation on an annual basis every July 1.

The base value of the CCTB stands at $1,307 beginning July 2008 (up from $1,283), with a $91 supplement (up from $90) added for a third and subsequent qualified child.

The CCTB benefit begins to be phased out at 2 per cent of family net income above $37,885 (up from $37,178 in 2007) for one dependent child, and 4 per cent of family net income (down from 5 per cent) above that threshold for two or more children.

Effective July 2008, the NCB supplement increased to $2,025 for the first child, $1,792 for the second child and $1,704 for each subsequent child (from $1,988, $1,758 and $1,673 respectively). The NCB supplement begins to reduce as net family income rises above $21,280 (up from $20,883).

As a result of the above changes, maximum annual combined CCTB benefits and NCB supplements increased to $3,332 for the first child, $3,099 for the second child and $3,102 for additional children (from $3,271 for the first child, $3,041 for the second child and $3,046 for each subsequent child).

The threshold level of net family income at which the NCB supplement is fully phased out has increased to $37,885 (from $37,178).

Both spouses/common-law partners must file an income tax return in order to receive the CCTB and NCB supplement.

Related child benefit amounts for Alberta, British Columbia, New Brunswick, Newfoundland and Labrador, the Northwest Territories, Nova Scotia, Nunavut, Ontario and the Yukon are also administered by the CRA.

Parents who are separated or divorced might each be eligible to receive a portion of the annual CCTB allotment on behalf of their dependant children if they share custody or even if the non-custodial parent temporarily resides with the children for at least one month during the year. The parent with whom the child resided on the first day of the month is generally considered to be eligible for their care and upbringing, and therefore eligible for the benefit.

See Appendix II on page 200 for details.

## Child Disability Benefit

The federal government introduced a Child Disability Benefit (CDB) in its 2003 federal budget. Effective July 1, 2007, it provides parents of children that have a disability with a supplement to the CCTB of up to $2,395 annually (up from $2,351 for the previous 12 months) per qualified child. In order to be eligible to receive this credit, their child must have a medical condition that qualifies them for the disability tax credit.

The full $2,395 benefit for the first eligible child is phased out at 2 per cent of family income in excess of the NCB supplement threshold limit of $37,885 (up from $31,178 for the previous 12 months). Thus, families who have one child who qualifies for both the full NCB supplement and Child Disability Benefit will receive a total annual CCTB benefit of $5,727 on behalf of that child for the 12 months beginning July 1, 2008.

The CDB is eliminated completely when the net income of a family responsible for one child that has a disability reaches $157,635. That limit will be higher if more children with disabilities are being cared for.

The disability credit may also be claimed with respect to certain dependants, provided they don't require the credit to reduce their own tax liability after claiming personal, age, pension credits and any credits relative to EI and CPP premiums paid.

The list of relatives to whom the unused portion of an individual's disability tax credit may be transferred under certain circumstances includes a parent, grandparent, child, grandchild, brother, sister, aunt, uncle, nephew or niece of that individual or their spouse/common-law partner, provided the individual with a disability is living with the supporting person and is at least partially dependent on them.

## Universal Child Care Benefit (UCCB)

The 2006 federal budget presented Canadians with a Universal Child Care Benefit (UCCB). The UCCB, which took effect July 1, 2006, provides all families in Canada with $100 per month, or $1,200 per year, for each child under the age of six. It is taxable in the hands of the lower-income spouse or common-law partner. Amounts received under the UCCB will not adversely affect income-tested federal benefits receivable such as old age security or employment insurance.

Families with eligible children that already receive the CCTB automatically receive the UCCB benefit. Those that do not will have to apply to the CRA.

## Old Age Security (OAS)

The maximum old age security pension amount payable to senior citizens in 2008 is approximately $6,049. At this rate, however, a clawback provision reduces old age security (OAS) pensions for individuals with net income exceeding $64,718. The clawback rate of 15 per cent eliminates the entire OAS benefit at $105,045 of net income.

The OAS is available to most Canadians at age 65. Check with the Human Resources and Social Development Canada (HRSDC) website at www.hrsdc.gc.ca for a more complete description regarding eligibility requirements.

## Guaranteed Income Supplement (GIS)

The guaranteed income supplement (GIS) is paid to individuals age 65 or over who qualify based on low income. GIS receipts are included in net income, affecting tax calculations, although an offsetting deduction allows individuals to exclude GIS benefits from taxable income.

## Alternative Minimum Tax (AMT)

The Alternative Minimum Tax (AMT) provision, which was introduced in 1986, has in past years imposed a minimum tax where little or no income tax is otherwise payable in a year due to the use of tax shelter losses, transfers to RRSPs or RPPs and various other tax provisions.

As a result of changes introduced in the 1998 federal budget, however, RRSP and RPP contributions, including those arising from the rollover of a retiring allowance, are now exempt from calculations that generate AMT. AMT triggered after 1993 as a result of RRSP and RPP contributions is refundable.

Individuals are generally subject to AMT in situations where the AMT exceeds ordinary taxes payable. AMT is computed on adjusted taxable income in excess of $40,000 at the lowest federal tax rate of 15 per cent (with credits allowed for certain personal amounts), plus the applicable provincial/territorial tax, as follows:

In Alberta, the AMT rate for 2008 is calculated at 35 per cent of the corresponding federal AMT. This amount is added to Alberta tax.

In British Columbia, the AMT rate for 2008 is calculated at 33.73 per cent of the corresponding federal AMT. This amount is added to British Columbia tax.

In Manitoba, the AMT rate for 2008 is calculated at 50 per cent of the corresponding federal AMT. This amount is added to Manitoba tax.

In New Brunswick, the AMT rate for 2008 is calculated at 57 per cent of the corresponding federal AMT. This amount is added to New Brunswick tax.

In Newfoundland and Labrador, the AMT rate for 2008 is calculated at 54.67 per cent of the corresponding federal AMT. This amount is added to Newfoundland and Labrador tax.

In the Northwest Territories, the AMT rate for 2008 is calculated at 45 per cent of the corresponding federal AMT. This amount is added to Northwest Territories tax.

In Nova Scotia, the AMT rate for 2008 is calculated at 57.50 per cent of the corresponding federal AMT. This amount is added to Nova Scotia tax.

In Nunavut, the AMT rate for 2008 is calculated at 45 per cent of the corresponding federal AMT. This amount is added to Nunavut tax.

In Ontario, the AMT rate for 2008 is calculated at 40.33 per cent of the corresponding federal AMT. This amount is added to Ontario tax.

In Prince Edward Island, the AMT rate for 2008 is calculated at 57.50 per cent of the corresponding federal AMT. This amount is added to Prince Edward Island tax.

In Quebec, the AMT rate for 2008 is calculated at 16 per cent, based on provincial AMT rules that provide for a basic exemption of $40,000 to be applied against adjusted taxable income for some individuals. Special rules apply. Consult a Certified General Accountant if you reside in the province and think the AMT may apply to you.

In Saskatchewan, the AMT rate for 2008 is calculated at 50 per cent of the corresponding federal AMT. This amount is added to Saskatchewan tax.

In the Yukon, the AMT rate for 2008 is calculated at 44 per cent of the corresponding federal AMT. This amount is added to Yukon tax.

Individuals may be liable to pay AMT if the following items are on their tax return:

- taxable dividends;
- a federal political contribution;
- the overseas employment tax credit;
- a labour-sponsored fund tax credit;
- taxable capital gains;
- a loss from a multiple-unit residential building (MURB) or certified film where CCA is taken;
- net losses from resource properties;
- employee stock options or share deductions;
- an employee home relocation deduction; or
- any losses or carrying charges arising from limited partnerships or investments identified as tax shelters.

AMT paid in excess of ordinary tax in one year is eligible to be carried forward seven years and deducted against tax payable in excess of the AMT liability in future years.

An individual who makes quarterly tax instalments is required to take the AMT into account for the purpose of determining instalments payable. This minimum tax is not applicable in the year of death.

## Foreign Pensions

Individuals who reside in Canada must normally pay Canadian tax on any pension income received from a foreign country in excess of C$1,000. Certain deductions may be allowed to avoid double taxation with the host country as determined by the existence of any tax conventions between Canada and that other country. Other conditions might also apply. For instance, Canada's tax agreement with Germany stipulates that social security benefits cannot be taxed more in the receiving country than had the recipient resided in the paying country.

Canada has tax conventions with close to 90 countries around the world. Taxpayers with ties to another nation who have questions about their tax status should consult their Certified General Accountant.

## United States Filing Requirements

The United States imposes tax and/or filing requirements on Canadians in certain circumstances.

Canadians who are considered residents for U.S. income tax purposes are subject to U.S. tax on their world income. Canadians are also required to report to the Internal Revenue Service (IRS) any U.S.-source income not subject to withholding tax, such as rental income earned on a condominium.

U.S. residency is determined on the basis of either immigration status or physical presence. The substantial presence test uses a formula taking into account the number of days individuals are present in the country during the current year, along with a fraction of the days they were present during the two preceding years.

Canadians who are considered U.S. residents under the substantial presence test, but are not in the U.S. for more than 182 days during the year, can avoid being considered residents for tax purposes by filing a closer connection statement. To qualify, individuals must show that closer connections to Canada exist, substantiated by the location of a permanent home or business establishment, as well as factors such as family and other social relationships.

Even taxpayers who maintain significant residential ties to the U.S. or another country might still be considered to be a Canadian resident for tax purposes, depending on a number of factors such as their length of stay in Canada — whether it is for a substantial period of time, or is occasional or intermittent, for instance: physical and/or financial property owned; maintenance of health coverage; driver's licence; existence of a bank account; and personal or business connections here.

The Canada-United States Tax Treaty determines residency for U.S. tax purposes for Canadians who are present in the U.S. in excess of 182 days. Taxpayers with dual citizenship in both Canada and the United States may also be subject to special rules. In certain instances, an apportionment of income earned in both countries might be required.

Complex taxation rules might also apply in situations where an individual is moving from one country to the other.

Check with your Certified General Accountant to determine your income tax filing requirements if you have ties to both countries.

## Tax Tips

The international location of a permanent home or business establishment will significantly affect both personal and corporate taxes. Therefore, a tax accountant and/or lawyer should be consulted if there is any ambiguity in this area.

An increasing number of Canadians own vacation property in the United States. Several complex tax issues, including estate related matters, could result on both sides of the border depending on factors such as joint ownership with a spouse and/or others (i.e., time sharing), especially if there is any commercial use associated with that property. Consult your Certified General Accountant to sort these matters out.

## Instalments

Instalments are required from self-employed taxpayers, or those whose taxes have not otherwise been withheld by their employer, if the difference between tax payable and amounts withheld at source is greater than $3,000 ($1,800 for residents of Quebec) in both the current and either of the two preceding years (for farmers and fishers, both of the two preceding years).

Quarterly instalments are due on the 15th of March, June, September and December (for farmers and fishers, one instalment only is due on December 31).

The total required instalment amount is equal to the preceding year's tax payable or estimated current year's tax payable, if lower. (For farmers and fishers, the instalment payable is two-thirds of this amount.)

The CRA sends instalment reminders based on a formula — with the first two instalments based on half of the second preceding year's net tax payable plus CPP contributions payable and the last two instalments based on the preceding year's tax and CPP (minus the first two instalments already paid during the current year). Alternatively, taxpayers may choose to pay all four instalments on the basis of the preceding year's tax payable if they feel that is more advantageous.

Interest is compounded daily and charged on late or deficient instalments at a prescribed rate (refer to Appendix VI, page 214, as well as Appendix VII, page 217). If the interest on deficient instalments is more than $1,000, an additional penalty of 50 per cent on that excess may apply. If instalments are paid according to the CRA's instalment reminders, no liability for interest or penalty will be assessed.

## Tax Tips

If your instalment has been late or deficient in the past, consider prepaying or overpaying future instalments. The CRA will offset interest on early or excess instalments against interest charged for the same year (although interest on any net balance will not be paid).

## Penalties and Interest Charges on Overdue Taxes

Individual taxpayers who do not file their returns by April 30 of the subsequent year (June 15 if they or their spouse or common-law partner have self-employed income) may be required to pay a late filing penalty. This penalty is 5 per cent of the balance owing, plus 1 per cent for each month the return is late up to a maximum of 12 months (with a maximum potential penalty of 17 per cent).

An additional penalty applies when returns are filed late and taxpayers have already received a late filing penalty during any of the three preceding years. This repeater penalty is equal to 10 per cent of the tax owing at the due date plus 2 per cent each month the return is late, up to 20 months (and a maximum potential penalty of 50 per cent).

Interest is charged on unpaid tax and penalties from the due date. Where there is self-employment income, the due date of the tax return is deferred to June 15; however, the balance of tax remains due on April 30 and interest will be charged on any balance owing from that date. This interest, charged at a prescribed rate, is compounded daily (refer to Appendix VI, page 214, as well as Appendix VII, page 217). Penalties and interest paid are not tax deductible.

Interest received from the CRA is taxable in the year of receipt.

## Tax Tips

To avoid penalties, file your return on time even if you are unable to pay the tax balance due.

## Taxpayer Relief Provisions

This series of legislation, previously known as the Fairness Package, allows the CRA to use discretion under certain circumstances in the following areas:

- with respect to the acceptance of late, amended or revoked elections;

- to waive or cancel part or all of a penalty or interest where taxpayers have not complied with a requirement under the *Income Tax Act* or applicable regulation because of extraordinary circumstances beyond their control; and

- to reassess or make a redetermination on an income tax return to give a refund, or to apply a refund against amounts owing beyond the normal three year period.

Details are outlined in CRA Information Circular IC07-1 — *Taxpayer Relief Provisions,* which replaces and consolidates the information in previous information circulars IC92-1, 92-2 and 92-3. This can be found at the URL: http://www.cra-arc.gc.ca/E/pub/tp/ic07-1/README.html, or in French at http://www.cra-arc.gc.ca/F/pub/tp/ic07-1.

The period in which a taxpayer may make a request to the CRA for relief under the above provisions is limited to 10 years from the end of the calendar year corresponding to the tax year or fiscal period in question.

Taxpayers can make their requests in writing to a district office or taxation centre with all relevant information, including their name, address, social insurance number, the applicable taxation year(s) and documents to support the application, including records of dates, times and names of people from whom information was received. If they believe the agency has not exercised its discretion in a fair and reasonable manner, they may request — in writing — that the director of the district office or taxation centre review their situation.

The CRA website at www.cra-arc.gc.ca contains a link to the CRA's voluntary-disclosures program (VDP), which provides a description of the program, including the circumstances upon which VDP relief from penalty and persecution may be considered.

The CRA also provides an online service called My Account, which is accessible through the main site. This allows individuals to access their personal income-tax-related information. They can access this site by providing their date of birth, social insurance number, income from their tax return and special web-access user name and password.

Information about taxpayer objection and appeal rights is also online; see document P148, entitled *Resolving Your Dispute: Objection and Appeal Rights Under the Income Tax Act*, accessible through the main CRA website.

## Tax Tips

Relief provisions might apply to certain areas in Canada when a natural disaster affects taxpayers' ability to file their returns on time. In 2008, for instance, the CRA provided relief with respect to penalties and interest for certain New Brunswick residents who were affected by flooding around the April 30 deadline.

Electronic financial records, preferably along with backup, must be retained for audit purposes, even if you have already printed off hard copies of such documents. Check with the Canada Revenue Agency regarding the appropriate minimum retention period.

Taxpayers who wish to file a notice of objection with respect to a CRA assessment must do so in writing, providing all relevant details. It is also vitally important that they adhere to all deadlines established by the CRA.

Taxpayers who would like to authorize a third party, such as another family member or a professional financial advisor like a Certified General Accountant, to deal with the CRA on their behalf, including online, can do so by filling out Form T1013 — *Authorizing or Cancelling a Representative*. They can log on to http://www.cra-arc.gc.ca/esrvc-srvce/tx/ndvdls/myccnt/menu-eng.html in English or http://www.cra-arc.gc.ca/esrvc-srvce/tx/ndvdls/myccnt/menu-fra.html in French.

## Taxpayer Alert Initiative

In late 2005, the CRA launched the Taxpayer Alert Initiative, which appears on the website http://www.cra-arc.gc.ca/gncy/lrt/menu-eng.html in English and http://www.cra-arc.gc.ca/gncy/lrt/menu-fra.html in French. This program offers concentrated information on a variety of tax-related topics, including unsavoury tax-avoidance schemes; the serious consequences associated with tax evasion; tax shelters and havens; and a description of how the underground economy hurts Canadians.

The website also contains tips on how to become an informed donor to charities; information about how the CRA conducts audits and investigations, including what taxpayers need to know if they are being audited; and a description of fairness and taxpayer rights, among a multitude of other topics.

## Taxpayer Bill of Rights

In May 2007, the CRA and federal Department of Finance announced the release of a Taxpayer Bill of Rights, which includes 15 rights about issues ranging from service, privacy, and procedures dealing with tax disputes, among others, plus an additional five commitments to small businesses in Canada.

The establishment of a Taxpayers' Ombudsman, to "operate independently and at arm's length from the CRA" was also announced. Among other duties, the mandate of this office is to "conduct impartial and independent reviews of service-related complaints about the CRA."

Details about both the Taxpayer Bill of Rights and Taxpayers' Ombudsman are available on the CRA website at www.cra-arc.gc.ca/menu-e.html in English and www.cra-arc.gc.ca/menu-fra.html in French.

## Notice of Objection

Taxpayers who disagree with the assessment they receive on their income tax return can formally object to the findings by writing to the Chief of Appeals at their Tax Services Office or Tax Centre. Alternatively, they can fill out a Form T400A — *Objection — Income Tax Act*. The time limit for individual taxpayers to file this objection is the later of: 90 days after the mailing date of the Notice of Assessment, or one year after the taxpayer's filing due date (accompanied by a written application, made on a timely basis, to the Canada Revenue Agency).

For GST objections, taxpayers can complete and mail Form GST159 — *Notice of Objection (GST/HST)* to the Chief of Appeals at their Tax Services Office. This must be done within 90 days of the mailing of their *Notice of Assessment* or *Notice of Determination*.

The Tax Court of Canada (TCC) is the first judicial level to which a tax dispute can be taken. Subsequent appeals of a TCC judgment must then be made to the Federal Court of Appeal (FCA) within 30 days of the decision being announced (excluding July and August). The final potential spot to resolve a dispute is with the Supreme Court of Canada; however, the Supreme Court must first approve the cases it hears and in practice only a small percentage of applications will be allowed to present to the nation's highest court.

## Estate Planning

An individual is deemed to have disposed of all assets owned, at fair market value, on their date of death. Estate planning can minimize tax consequences at death by implementing specific tax deferral measures in advance. Such measures include inter-spousal rollovers of assets, rollovers to corporations, the creation of family trusts and estate freezes.

Since estate tax planning is complex and beyond the scope of this tax-planning book, consider seeking professional advice from your Certified General Accountant.

# CONCLUSION

Tax planning is always necessary — particularly under an income tax system such as Canada's that incorporates a progressive rate schedule with rules that allow or disallow specific transactions and courses of action.

Furthermore, new federal and provincial laws and policies are constantly being introduced; these often have a direct effect on specific tax strategies, because new opportunities may arise and old approaches may no longer be appropriate or valid as a result. It is, therefore, incumbent upon taxpayers to remain aware of contemporary tax rules that are applicable to specific actions being contemplated.

For these reasons, it is also a good idea to review any tax-planning proposals with a Certified General Accountant.

Link to Canada Revenue Agency, NETFILE:

Canada Revenue Agency has developed a new and highly secure online personal income tax filing service called NETFILE.

By using NETFILE certified tax preparation software, individuals can file personal income tax returns online. Visit www.netfile.gc.ca to file your return or for more information.

# APPENDICES

# APPENDIX I

## Personal Tax Credits

| Description | Federal Rates | | Alberta Rates | |
| --- | --- | --- | --- | --- |
| | 2008 Federal Amount | Maximum Federal Credit [1] | 2008 Provincial Amount | Maximum Provincial Credit [1] |
| Basic credit | $9,600 | $1,440 | $16,161 | $1,616 |
| Employment credit | 1,019 | 153 | 0 | 0 |
| Spousal credit [2] | 9,600 | 1,440 | 16,161 | 1,616 |
| – reduced by net income over $0 (federally) | | | | |
| – reduced by net income over $0 (Alberta) | | | | |
| Equivalent-to-spouse credit [2] | 9,600 | 1,440 | 16,161 | 1,616 |
| – reduced by net income over $0 (federally) | | | | |
| – reduced by net income over $0 (Alberta) | | | | |
| Age credit – over 64 [3][4] | 5,276 | 791 | 4,503 | 450 |
| – reduced by net income over $31,524 (federally) | | | | |
| – reduced by net income over $33,525 (Alberta) | | | | |
| Disability credit [5] | 7,021 | 1,053 | 12,466 | 1,247 |
| Disability supplement for child under 18 and dependent by reason of mental or physical infirmity [2] | 4,095 | 614 | 9,355 | 936 |
| – reduced by child care and attendant care expenses over $2,399 (federally) | | | | |
| – reduced by child care and attendant care expenses over $2,552 (Alberta) | | | | |
| Dependants 18 and over and dependent by reason of mental or physical infirmity [2] | 4,095 | 614 | 9,355 | 936 |
| – reduced by net income over $5,811 (federally) | | | | |
| – reduced by net income over $6,180 (Alberta) | | | | |

| | | | | |
|---|---|---|---|---|
| Caregiver amount [2] | 4,095 | 614 | 9,355 | 936 |
| – reduced by net income over $13,986 (federally) | | | | |
| – reduced by net income over $14,874 (Alberta) | | | | |
| Adoption amount | 10,643 | 1,596 | 11,053 | 1,105 |
| Child tax credit (under 18 years) | 2,038 | 306 | 0 | 0 |
| Children's fitness | 500 | 75 | 0 | 0 |
| Eligible medical expenses, | each 100 | 15 | 100 | 10 |
| – less 3% of net income to a maximum of $1,962 (federally) and $2,088 (Alberta) | | | | |
| Tuition credit [6] [7] | each 100 | 15 | 100 | 10 |
| Education credit per month of qualified attendance [7] | | | | |
| – full time | 400 | 60 | 628* | 63 |
| – part time | 120 | 18 | 188* | 19 |
| Textbook credit per month of qualified attendance | | | | |
| – full time | 65 | 10 | 0 | 0 |
| – part time | 20 | 3 | 0 | 0 |
| Student loan interest credit | each 100 | 15 | 100 | 10 |
| Pension income received to a maximum of [4] | 2,000 | 300 | 1,244* | 124 |
| Donations | | | | |
| – first $200 | each 100 | 15 | 100 | 10 |
| – excess [8] | each 100 | 29 | 100 | 21 |
| Public transit pass | each 100 | 15 | 100 | 0 |
| CPP (premiums paid) [9] | 2,049 | 307 | 2,049 | 205 |
| EI (premiums paid) [10] | 711 | 107 | 711 | 71 |

* Education and pension amounts indexed in Alberta only.

| Description | British Columbia Rates | | Manitoba Rates | |
|---|---|---|---|---|
| | 2008 Provincial Amount | Maximum Provincial Credit [1] | 2008 Provincial Amount | Maximum Provincial Credit [1] |
| Basic credit | $9,189 | $465 | $8,034 | $ 876 |
| Employment credit | 0 | 0 | 0 | 0 |
| Spousal credit [2] | 7,868 | 398 | 8,034 | 876 |
| – reduced by net income over $787 (British Columbia) | | | | |
| – reduced by net income over $0 (Manitoba) | | | | |
| Equivalent-to-spouse credit [2] | 7,868 | 398 | 8,034 | 876 |
| – reduced by net income over $787 (British Columbia) | | | | |
| – reduced by net income over $0 (Manitoba) | | | | |
| Age credit – over 64 [3][4] | 4,121 | 209 | 3,728 | 406 |
| – reduced by net income over $30,674 (British Columbia) | | | | |
| – reduced by net income over $27,749 (Manitoba) | | | | |
| Disability credit [5] | 6,892 | 349 | 6,180 | 674 |
| Disability supplement for child under 18 and dependent by reason of mental or physical infirmity [2] | 4,021 | 203 | 3,605 | 393 |
| – reduced by child care and attendant care expenses over $2,334 (British Columbia) | | | | |
| – reduced by child care and attendant care expenses over $2,112 (Manitoba) | | | | |
| Dependants 18 and over and dependent by reason of mental or physical infirmity [2] | 4,021 | 203 | 3,605 | 393 |
| – reduced by net income over $6,405 (British Columbia) | | | | |
| – reduced by net income over $5,115 (Manitoba) | | | | |
| Caregiver amount [2] | 4,021 | 203 | 3,605 | 393 |
| – reduced by net income over $13,608 (British Columbia) | | | | |
| – reduced by net income over $12,312 (Manitoba) | | | | |

| | | | | |
|---|---|---|---|---|
| Adoption amount | 10,643 | 539 | 10,000 | 1,090 |
| Child tax credit (under 18 years) | 0 | 0 | 0 | 0 |
| Children's fitness | 0 | 0 | 500 | 55 |
| Eligible medical expenses | each 100 | 5.06 | 100 | 10.90 |

– less 3% of net income to a maximum of $1,911 (British Columbia) and $1,728 (Manitoba)

| | | | | |
|---|---|---|---|---|
| Tuition credit [6][7] | each 100 | 5.06 | 100 | 10.90 |

Education credit per month of qualified attendance [7]

| | | | | |
|---|---|---|---|---|
| – full time | 200 | 10 | 400 | 44 |
| – part time | 60 | 3 | 120 | 13 |

Textbook credit per month of qualified attendance

| | | | | |
|---|---|---|---|---|
| – full time | 0 | 0 | 0 | 0 |
| – part time | 0 | 0 | 0 | 0 |
| Student loan interest credit | each 100 | 5.06 | 100 | 10.90 |
| Pension income received to a maximum of [4] | 1,000 | 51 | 1,000 | 109 |

Donations

| | | | | |
|---|---|---|---|---|
| – first $200 | each 100 | 5.06 | 100 | 10.90 |
| – excess [8] | each 100 | 14.70 | 100 | 17.40 |
| Public transit pass | each 100 | 0 | 100 | 0 |
| CPP (premiums paid) [9] | 2,049 | 104 | 2,049 | 223 |
| EI (premiums paid) [10] | 711 | 36 | 711 | 78 |

| Description | New Brunswick Rates | | Newfoundland & Labrador Rates | |
|---|---|---|---|---|
| | 2008 Provincial Amount | Maximum Provincial Credit [1] | 2008 Provincial Amount | Maximum Provincial Credit [1] |
| Basic credit | $8,395 | $850 | $7,566 | $620 |
| Employment credit | 0 | 0 | 0 | 0 |
| Spousal credit [2] | 7,129 | 721 | 6,183 | 507 |

– reduced by net income over $713 (New Brunswick)
– reduced by net income over $619 (Newfoundland & Labrador)

| | | | | |
|---|---|---|---|---|
| Equivalent-to-spouse credit [2] | 7,129 | 721 | 6,183 | 507 |

– reduced by net income over $713 (New Brunswick)
– reduced by net income over $619 (Newfoundland & Labrador)

| | | | | |
|---|---|---|---|---|
| Age credit – over 64 [3][4] | 4,099 | 415 | 3,556 | 292 |

– reduced by net income over $30,517 (New Brunswick)
– reduced by net income over $26,468 (Newfoundland & Labrador)

| | | | | |
|---|---|---|---|---|
| Disability credit [5] | 6,797 | 688 | 5,106 | 419 |

| | | | | |
|---|---|---|---|---|
| Disability supplement for child under 18 and dependent by reason of mental or physical infirmity [2] | 3,965 | 401 | 2,402 | 197 |

– reduced by child care and attendant care expenses over $2,321 (New Brunswick)
– reduced by child care and attendant care expenses over $2,042 (Newfoundland & Labrador)

| | | | | |
|---|---|---|---|---|
| Dependants 18 and over and dependent by reason of mental or physical infirmity [2] | 3,965 | 401 | 2,402 | 197 |

– reduced by net income over $5,625 (New Brunswick)
– reduced by net income over $5,164 (Newfoundland & Labrador)

| | | | | |
|---|---|---|---|---|
| Caregiver amount [2] | 3,965 | 401 | 2,402 | 197 |

– reduced by net income over $13,540 (New Brunswick)
– reduced by net income over $11,743 (Newfoundland & Labrador)

| | | | | |
|---|---|---|---|---|
| Adoption amount | 0 | 0 | 10,211 | 837 |
| Child tax credit (under 18 years) | 0 | 0 | 0 | 0 |
| Children's fitness | 0 | 0 | 0 | 0 |
| Eligible medical expenses | each 100 | 10.12 | 100 | 8.20 |

– less 3% of net income to a maximum of \$1,899 (New Brunswick) and \$1,646 (Newfoundland & Labrador)

| | | | | |
|---|---|---|---|---|
| Tuition credit [6][7] | each 100 | 10.12 | 100 | 8.20 |

Education credit per month of qualified attendance [7]

| | | | | |
|---|---|---|---|---|
| – full time | 400 | 40 | 200 | 16 |
| – part time | 120 | 12 | 60 | 5 |

Textbook credit per month of qualified attendance

| | | | | |
|---|---|---|---|---|
| – full time | 0 | 0 | 0 | 0 |
| – part time | 0 | 0 | 0 | 0 |
| Student loan interest credit | each 100 | 10.12 | 100 | 8.20 |
| Pension income received to a maximum of [4] | 1,000 | 101 | 1,000 | 82 |

Donations

| | | | | |
|---|---|---|---|---|
| – first \$200 | each 100 | 10.12 | 100 | 8.20 |
| – excess [8] | each 100 | 17.95 | 100 | 16.00 |
| Public transit pass | each 100 | 0 | 100 | 0 |
| CPP (premiums paid) [9] | 2,049 | 207 | 2,049 | 168 |
| EI (premiums paid) [10] | 711 | 72 | 711 | 58 |

| Description | Northwest Territories Rates | | Nova Scotia Rates | |
|---|---|---|---|---|
| | 2008 Territorial Amount | Maximum Territorial Credit [1] | 2008 Provincial Amount | Maximum Provincial Credit [1] |
| Basic credit | $12,355 | $729 | $7,731 | $680 |
| Employment credit | 0 | 0 | 0 | 0 |
| Spousal credit [2] | 12,355 | 729 | 6,565 | 577 |
| – reduced by net income over $0 (Northwest Territories) | | | | |
| – reduced by net income over $656 (Nova Scotia) | | | | |
| Equivalent-to-spouse credit [2] | 12,355 | 729 | 6,565 | 577 |
| – reduced by net income over $0 (Northwest Territories) | | | | |
| – reduced by net income over $656 (Nova Scotia) | | | | |
| Age credit – over 64 [3][4] | 6,044 | 357 | 3,775 | 332 |
| – reduced by net income over $31,524 (Northwest Territories) | | | | |
| – reduced by net income over $28,101 (Nova Scotia) | | | | |
| Disability credit [5] | 10,020 | 591 | 4,596 | 404 |
| Disability supplement for child under 18 and dependent by reason of mental or physical infirmity [2] | 4,095 | 242 | 3,145 | 276 |
| – reduced by child care and attendant care expenses over $2,399 (Northwest Territories) | | | | |
| – reduced by child care and attendant care expenses over $2,139 (Nova Scotia) | | | | |
| Dependants 18 and over and dependent by reason of mental or physical infirmity [2] | 4,095 | 242 | 2,551 | 224 |
| – reduced by net income over $5,811 (Northwest Territories) | | | | |
| – reduced by net income over $5,180 (Nova Scotia) | | | | |
| Caregiver amount [2] | 4,095 | 242 | 4,465 | 392 |
| – reduced by net income over $13,986 (Northwest Territories) | | | | |
| – reduced by net income over $12,467 (Nova Scotia) | | | | |

| | | | | |
|---|---|---|---|---|
| Adoption amount | 0 | 0 | 0 | 0 |
| Child tax credit (under 18 years) | 0 | 0 | 0 | 0 |
| Children's fitness | 0 | 0 | 500 | 44 |

*Nova Scotia credit known as the Healthy Living Tax Incentive

| | | | | |
|---|---|---|---|---|
| Eligible medical expenses | each 100 | 5.90 | 100 | 8.79 |

– less 3% of net income to a maximum of $1,926 (Northwest Territories) and $1,637 (Nova Scotia)

| | | | | |
|---|---|---|---|---|
| Tuition credit [6][7] | each 100 | 5.90 | 100 | 8.79 |

Education credit per month of qualified attendance [7]

| | | | | |
|---|---|---|---|---|
| – full time | 400 | 24 | 200 | 18 |
| – part time | 120 | 7 | 60 | 5 |

Textbook credit per month of qualified attendance

| | | | | |
|---|---|---|---|---|
| – full time | 0 | 0 | 0 | 0 |
| – part time | 0 | 0 | 0 | 0 |
| Student loan interest credit | each 100 | 5.90 | 100 | 8.79 |
| Pension income received to a maximum of [4] | 1,000 | 59 | 1,069* | 94 |
| Donations | | | | |
| – first $200 | each 100 | 5.90 | 100 | 8.79 |
| – excess [8] | each 100 | 14.05 | 100 | 17.50 |
| Public transit pass | each 100 | 0 | 100 | 0 |
| CPP (premiums paid) [9] | 2,049 | 121 | 2,049 | 180 |
| EI (premiums paid) [10] | 711 | 42 | 711 | 62 |

* Pension amount indexed in Nova Scotia.

| Description | Nunavut Rates | | Ontario Rates | |
| --- | --- | --- | --- | --- |
| | 2008 Territorial Amount | Maximum Territorial Credit [1] | 2008 Provincial Amount | Maximum Provincial Credit [1] |
| Basic credit | $11,360 | $454 | $8,681 | $525 |
| Employment credit | 0 | 0 | 0 | 0 |
| Spousal credit [2] | 11,360 | 454 | 7,371 | 446 |
| – reduced by net income over $0 (Nunavut) | | | | |
| – reduced by net income over $737 (Ontario) | | | | |
| Equivalent-to-spouse credit [2] | 11,360 | 454 | 7,371 | 446 |
| – reduced by net income over $0 (Nunavut) | | | | |
| – reduced by net income over $737 (Ontario) | | | | |
| Age credit | | | | |
| – over 64 [3][4] | 8,520 | 341 | 4,239 | 256 |
| – reduced by net income over $31,524 (Nunavut) | | | | |
| – reduced by net income over $31,554 (Ontario) | | | | |
| Disability credit [5] | 11,360 | 454 | 7,014 | 424 |
| Disability supplement for child under 18 and dependent by reason of mental or physical infirmity [2] | 4,095 | 164 | 4,091 | 248 |
| – reduced by child care and attendant care expenses over $2,399 (Nunavut) | | | | |
| – reduced by child care and attendant care expenses over $2,396 (Ontario) | | | | |
| Dependants 18 and over and dependent by reason of mental or physical infirmity [2] | 4,095 | 164 | 4,091 | 248 |
| – reduced by net income over $5,811 (Nunavut) | | | | |
| – reduced by net income over $5,817 (Ontario) | | | | |
| Caregiver amount [2] | 4,095 | 164 | 4,092 | 248 |
| – reduced by net income over $13,986 (Nunavut) | | | | |
| – reduced by net income over $13,999 (Ontario) | | | | |

| | | | | |
|---|---|---|---|---|
| Adoption amount | 0 | 0 | 10,591 | 641 |
| Child tax credit (under 18 years) | 0 | 0 | 0 | 0 |
| Children's fitness | 0 | 0 | 0 | 0 |
| Eligible medical expenses | each 100 | 4 | 100 | 6.05 |
| – less 3% of net income to a maximum of $1,962 (Nunavut) and $1,965 (Ontario) | | | | |
| Tuition credit [6][7] | each 100 | 4 | 100 | 6.05 |
| Education credit per month of qualified attendance [7] | | | | |
| – full time | 400 | 16 | 468* | 28 |
| – part time | 120 | 5 | 140* | 8 |
| Textbook credit per month of qualified attendance | | | | |
| – full time | 65 | 3 | 0 | 0 |
| – part time | 20 | 1 | 0 | 0 |
| Student loan interest credit | each 100 | 4 | 100 | 6.05 |
| Pension income received to a maximum of [4] | 2,000 | 80 | 1,201* | 73 |
| Donations | | | | |
| – first $200 | each 100 | 4 | 100 | 6.05 |
| – excess [8] | each 100 | 11.50 | 100 | 11.16 |
| Public transit pass | each 100 | 0 | 100 | 0 |
| CPP (premiums paid) [9] | 2,049 | 82 | 2,049 | 124 |
| EI (premiums paid) [10] | 711 | 28 | 711 | 43 |

\* Education and pension amounts indexed in Ontario.

| Description | Prince Edward Island Rates | | Quebec Rates | |
|---|---|---|---|---|
| | 2008 Provincial Amount | Maximum Provincial Credit [1] | 2008 Provincial Amount | Maximum Provincial Credit [1] |
| Basic credit | $7,708 | $755 | $10,215 | $2,043 |
| Employment credit | 0 | 0 | 0 | 0 |
| Spousal credit [2] | 6,546 | 642 | N/A | N/A |
| – reduced by net income over $655 (Prince Edward Island) | | | | |
| Equivalent-to-spouse credit [2] | 6,294 | 617 | N/A | N/A |
| – reduced by net income over $629 (Prince Edward Island) | | | | |
| Age credit – over 64 [3][4] | 3,764 | 369 | 2,200 | 440 |
| – reduced by net income over $28,019 (Prince Edward Island) | | | | |
| – reduced by net family income over $29,645 (Quebec) | | | | |
| Disability credit [5] | 6,890 | 675 | 2,325 | 465 |
| Disability supplement for child under 18 and dependent by reason of mental or physical infirmity [2] | 4,019 | 394 | N/A | N/A |
| – reduced by child care and attendant care expenses over $2,354 (Prince Edward Island) | | | | |
| Dependants 18 and over and dependent by reason of mental or physical infirmity [2] | 2,446 | 240 | N/A | N/A |
| – reduced by net income over $4,966 (Prince Edward Island) | | | | |
| Dependants 18 and over (non-students)   see above | | | 2,740 | 548 |
| – reduced by 80 per cent of net income, determined regardless of any scholarships, fellowships or awards (Quebec) | | | | |
| Caregiver amount [2] | 2,446 | 240 | | 1,033 (Refundable) |
| – reduced by net income over $11,953 (Prince Edward Island) | | | | |
| – reduced by net income over $20,650 (Quebec) | | | | |
| 2nd refundable caregiver amount | | | 5,200 | 1,560 |
| -reduced by 3 per cent of family income over $50,000 (Quebec) | | | | |

| | | | | |
|---|---|---|---|---|
| Adoption amount | 0 | 0 | 20,000 | 10,000* |
| Child tax credit (under 18 years) | 0 | 0 | 0 | 0 |
| Children's fitness | 0 | 0 | 0 | 0 |
| Eligible medical expenses, | each 100 | 9.80 | 100 | 20 |
| – less 3% of net income to a maximum of $1,678 (Prince Edward Island) | | | | |
| – less 3% of family income (Quebec) | | | | |
| Tuition credit [6][7][8] | each 100 | 9.80 | see notes | |
| Education credit per month of qualified attendance [7] | | | | |
| – full time | 400 | 39 | N/A | N/A |
| – part time | 120 | 12 | N/A | N/A |
| Textbook credit per month of qualified attendance | | | | |
| – full time | 0 | 0 | N/A | N/A |
| – part time | 0 | 0 | N/A | N/A |
| Student loan interest credit | each 100 | 9.80 | 100 | 20 |
| Pension income received to a maximum of [4] | 1,000 | 98 | 1,500 | 300 |
| – reduced by net family income over $29,645 (Quebec) | | | | |
| Donations | | | | |
| – first $200 | each 100 | 9.80 | 100 | 20 |
| – excess | each 100 | 16.70 | 100 | 24** |
| Public transit pass | each 100 | 0 | 100 | 0 |
| CPP/QPP (premiums paid) [9] | 2,049 | 201 | 2,049 | — |
| EI (premiums paid) [9][11] | 711 | 70 | 571 | — |
| QPIP (premiums paid) [10][11] | | 272 | | — |

\* Credit also available for certain medical treatments for infertility.
\*\* For Quebec residents, donations over $200 attract a tax credit of 24 per cent.

| Description | Saskatchewan Rates | | Yukon Rates | |
|---|---|---|---|---|
| | 2008 Provincial Amount | Maximum Provincial Credit [1] | 2008 Territorial Amount | Maximum Territorial Credit [1] |
| Basic credit | $12,945 | $1,424 | $9,600 | $ 676 |
| Employment credit | 0 | 0 | 1,019 | 72 |
| Spousal credit [2] | 12,945 | 1,424 | 9,600 | 676 |
| – reduced by net income over $895 (Saskatchewan) | | | | |
| – reduced by net income over $0 (Yukon) | | | | |
| Equivalent-to-spouse credit [2] | 12,945 | 1,424 | 9,600 | 676 |
| – reduced by net income over $895 (Saskatchewan) | | | | |
| – reduced by net income over $0 (Yukon) | | | | |
| Age credit – over 64 [3][4] | 4,235 | 466 | 5,276 | 371 |
| – reduced by net income over $31,524 (Saskatchewan) | | | | |
| – reduced by net income over $31,524 (Yukon) | | | | |
| Senior supplementary amount – over age 64 | 1,118 | 123 | N/A | N/A |
| Disability credit [5] | 8,190 | 901 | 7,021 | 494 |
| Disability supplement for child under 18 and dependent by reason of mental or physical infirmity [2] | 8,190 | 901 | 4,095 | 288 |
| – reduced by child care and attendant care expenses over $2,399 (Saskatchewan) | | | | |
| – reduced by child care and attendant care expenses over $2,399 (Yukon) | | | | |
| Dependants 18 and over and dependent by reason of mental or physical infirmity [2] | 8,190 | 901 | 4,095 | 288 |
| – reduced by net income over $5,811 (Saskatchewan) | | | | |
| – reduced by net income over $5,811 (Yukon) | | | | |
| Caregiver amount [2] | 8,190 | 901 | 4,095 | 288 |
| – reduced by net income over $13,986 (Saskatchewan) | | | | |
| – reduced by net income over $13,986 (Yukon) | | | | |

| | | | | |
|---|---|---|---|---|
| Adoption amount | 0 | 0 | 10,643 | 749 |
| Child tax credit (under 18 years) | 4,795 | 527 | 2,038 | 143 |
| Children's fitness | 0 | 0 | 500 | 35 |
| Eligible medical expenses, | each 100 | 11 | 100 | 7.04 |
| – less 3 per cent of net income to a maximum of $1,962 (Saskatchewan) and $1,962 (Yukon) | | | | |
| Tuition credit [6][7] | each 100 | 11 | 100 | 7.04 |
| Education credit per month of qualified attendance [7] | | | | |
| – full time | 400 | 44 | 400 | 28 |
| – part time | 120 | 13 | 120 | 8 |
| Textbook credit per month of qualified attendance | | | | |
| – full time | 0 | 0 | 65 | 5 |
| – part time | 0 | 0 | 20 | 1 |
| Student loan interest credit | each 100 | 11 | 100 | 7.04 |
| Pension income received to a maximum of [4] | 1,000 | 110 | 2,000 | 141 |
| Donations | | | | |
| – first $200 | each 100 | 11 | 100 | 7.04 |
| – excess [8] | each 100 | 15 | 100 | 12.76 |
| Public transit pass | each 100 | 0 | 100 | 7.04 |
| CPP (premiums paid) [9] | 2,049 | 225 | 2,049 | 144 |
| EI (premiums paid) [10] | 711 | 78 | 711 | 50 |

Most personal tax credits, including the basic, spousal and equivalent-to-spouse, medical dependency, disability and age tax credits, are fully indexed to the annual inflation rate, as determined by the applicable Consumer Price Index (CPI) rates. Indexation is designed to prevent

Canadian taxpayers from ending up in a higher tax bracket solely because of an inflation-induced increase in salary.

Items marked with an asterisk (*) are indexed in Alberta, Nova Scotia and Ontario only.

(1)  Federal credits calculated at 15 per cent of gross amount, except donations over $200, which are calculated at 29 per cent. Provincial/territorial credits calculated at lowest tax amount, except for donations over $200, whose totals are calculated at the highest taxation amount in that jurisdiction — see Appendix III for rates. Quebec credits are calculated at 20 per cent of the gross amount, except donations over $200, which are calculated at 24 per cent. Both credits apply to reduce basic tax, before surtaxes, and have a higher real value if surtaxes otherwise apply.

(2)  Where the dependants' net income is in excess of the indicated threshold, such excess will decrease the gross amount for purposes of calculating the credit amount.

The federal portion of the spousal and equivalent-to-spouse credits is eliminated when net income reaches $9,600. The provincial/territorial portion of these credits is eliminated when net income reaches:net income reaches:

- in Alberta: $16,161
- British Columbia: $8,655
- Manitoba: $8,034
- New Brunswick: $7,842
- Newfoundland & Labrador: $6,802
- Northwest Territories: $12,355
- Nova Scotia: $7,221
- Nunavut: $11,360
- Ontario: $8,108
- Prince Edward Island: $7,201 (spousal only); $6,923 for equivalent-to-spouse
- Quebec: N/A
- Saskatchewan: $13,840
- Yukon: $9,600

The federal portion of the disability supplement for children under 18 is eliminated when child care and attendant care expenses reach $6,494. The provincial/territorial portion of this credit is eliminated when net income reaches:

- in Alberta: $11,907
- British Columbia: $6,355

- Manitoba: $5,717
- New Brunswick: $6,286
- Newfoundland & Labrador: $4,444
- Northwest Territories: $6,494
- Nova Scotia: $5,284
- Nunavut: $6,494
- Ontario: $6,487
- Prince Edward Island: $6,373
- Quebec: N/A
- Saskatchewan: $10,589
- Yukon: $6,494

The federal portion of the infirm dependant credit is eliminated when net income reaches $9,906. The provincial/territorial portion of this credit is eliminated when net income reaches:

- in Alberta: $15,535
- British Columbia: $10,426
- Manitoba: $8,720
- New Brunswick: $9,590
- Newfoundland & Labrador: $7,566
- Northwest Territories: $9,906
- Nova Scotia: $7,731
- Nunavut: $9,906
- Ontario: $9,908
- Prince Edward Island: $7,412
- Quebec: $3,425 (non-students only)
- Saskatchewan: $14,001
- Yukon: $9,906

With the caregiver amount, the federal credit is eliminated when net income reaches $18,081. The provincial/territorial portion is eliminated when net income reaches:

- in Alberta: $24,229
- British Columbia: $17,629
- Manitoba: $15,917
- New Brunswick: $17,505
- Newfoundland & Labrador: $14,145
- Northwest Territories: $18,081
- Nova Scotia: $16,932
- Nunavut: $18,081
- Ontario: $18,091

- Prince Edward Island: $14,399
- Quebec: N/A
- Saskatchewan: $22,176
- Yukon: $18,081

(3) The federal credit for age amount is reduced by 15 per cent of net income over $31,524. The federal portion of this credit is therefore eliminated when net income reaches $66,697. The provincial/territorial credit for age amount is reduced by 15 per cent of net income over:

- in Alberta: $33,525
- British Columbia: $30,674
- Manitoba: $27,749
- New Brunswick: $30,517
- Newfoundland & Labrador: $26,468
- Northwest Territories: $31,524
- Nova Scotia: $28,101
- Nunavut: $31,524
- Ontario: $31,554
- Prince Edward Island: $28,019
- Quebec: Combined with the amount for retirement income and the amount for a person living alone with the corresponding amounts, as the case may be, of which the individual's spouse may take advantage, then total reduced by 15 per cent of net family income in excess of $29,645.
- Saskatchewan: $31,524
- Yukon: $31,524

The provincial/territorial portion of this credit is therefore eliminated when net income reaches:

- in Alberta: $63,545
- British Columbia: $58,147
- Manitoba: $52,602
- New Brunswick: $57,844
- Newfoundland & Labrador: $50,175
- Northwest Territories: $71,817
- Nova Scotia: $53,268
- Nunavut: $88,324
- Ontario: $59,814
- Prince Edward Island: $53,112
- Quebec: N/A (see above)

- Saskatchewan: $59,757
- Yukon: $66,697

(4) Age and pension credits may be transferred to a spouse or common-law partner to the extent not required by the taxpayer.

(5) Disability credits may be transferred to a supporting person (specifically to a spouse or common-law partner in Quebec) to the extent not required by that individual.

(6) Must exceed $100 per institution.

(7) Federal tuition and education credits to a maximum of 15 per cent of $5,000, and provincial/territorial tuition and education credits to a maximum of:

| | |
|---|---|
| – in Alberta: | 10.00 per cent of $5,000 |
| – British Columbia: | 5.06 per cent of $5,000 |
| – Manitoba: | 10.90 per cent of $5,000 |
| – New Brunswick: | 10.12 per cent of $5,000 |
| – Newfoundland & Labrador: | 8.20 per cent of $5,000 |
| – Northwest Territories: | 5.90 per cent of $5,000 |
| – Nova Scotia: | 8.79 per cent of $5,000 |
| – Nunavut: | 4.00 per cent of $5,000 |
| – Ontario: | 6.05 per cent of $6,003 (indexed) |
| – Prince Edward Island: | 9.80 per cent of $5,000 |
| – Quebec: | See Appendix Note #11 |
| – Saskatchewan: | 11.00 per cent of $5,000 |
| – Yukon: | 7.04 per cent of $5,000 |

may be transferred to a spouse or common-law partner, parent or grandparent to the extent not required by the student. Alternatively, unused credits can be carried forward indefinitely by the student, although the outstanding balance must be reduced in future years as soon as adequate income is earned to absorb the credits.

(8) To a maximum of 75 per cent of net income for all donations, including those made to the Crown or Crown agencies, except in the year of death or the immediately preceding year, when the ceiling is 100 per cent of net income.

(9) Employee and employer contribution rates for CPP pensionable earnings in 2008 are each assessed at 4.95 per cent of pensionable earnings up to a maximum of $44,900 (up from $43,700 in 2007), less a basic $3,500 exemption. Self-employed individuals

must pay both the employer and employee halves of this payment (a total of 9.9 per cent), but are entitled to a non-refundable tax credit for one-half of the premiums paid and a deduction from income for the other half.

(10) The employee portion of EI premiums is assessed at $1.73 per $100 of insurable earnings ($1.39 for Quebec residents) in 2008 to a maximum of $41,100 (up from $40,000 in 2007).

The employee portion of Quebec parental insurance plan (QPIP) premiums is assessed at 0.450 per $100 of insurable earnings in 2008 to a maximum of $60,500.

(11) A number of special rules apply to Quebec's personal tax credits. Among them:

– the age, pension and living alone credits are reduced if net family income exceeds $29,645;

– the QPP and EI credits shown in this Appendix are not available and are included in the complementary amount, which is used to calculate the basic amount;

– since 2006, the under 18 disability credit has been replaced by an increase in the monthly supplement to child assistance payments provided on behalf of children with disabilities;

– since 2006, the adult infirm dependant and caregiver credits have been combined into a refundable caregiver tax credit, with a maximum credit of $1,033 dependent on income available in 2008;

– in 2008, Quebec introduced a second refundable caregiver tax credit to cover respite expenses of informal caregivers provided to any person. It is worth up to 30 per cent on $5,200, for a maximum credit of $1,560, reduced by 3 per cent of family income in excess of $50,000.

– there is a maximum education credit of $377 per term, for up to two terms a year, available for a supporting parent of minor children; and

– in 2008, the tax credit for adult children who are students was replaced by the transfer to parents of the unused portion of the amount for recognized essential needs of the child, to a maximum of $6,730.

With respect to the basic credit for the 2008 taxation year, the basic amount that may be taken into account is $10,215, or the total of the following amounts, whichever is higher:

- the amount payable for the year by the taxpayer as employee premiums under the Employment Insurance Act and under the Act respecting parental insurance;
- the amount payable for the year by the taxpayer as employee contributions under the Act respecting the Quebec Pension Plan or an equivalent plan;
- the amount corresponding to 50 per cent of the amount payable for the year by the taxpayer as contributions on self-employment income under the Act respecting the Quebec Pension Plan or an equivalent plan;
- the portion of the amount payable as a premium by the tax-payer as a self-employed worker under the Act respecting parental insurance, represented by the ratio between the rate for determining the premium of an employee and the rate for determining the premium of a self-employed worker for the year; and
- the amount payable for the year by the taxpayer for the purposes of the one per cent contribution to the Health Services Fund (HSF).

Check with your Certified General Accountant to clarify your personal tax situation if you reside in Quebec.

# APPENDIX IA

## Ordering of Federal Non-Refundable Tax Credits

The *Income Tax Act* requires that the federal non-refundable tax credits be claimed in the following order:

- personal tax credits (i.e., basic personal tax credit, spousal and spousal equivalent tax credits, and dependant/caregiver tax credits);
- age credit for an individual who has attained the age of 65;
- credit for employee contributions to the CPP and employee premiums for EI;
- credit for an individual who is in receipt of certain pension income;
- credit for Canada employment income;
- credit for adoption expenses;
- credit for eligible long-term transit passes;
- credit for child fitness tax credit;
- credit for severe and prolonged mental or physical impairment of:
  - (i) an individual; or
  - (ii) a dependant
- credit for unused tuition, education and textbook tax credits;
- tuition credit for fees of a student enrolled at a designated educational institution;
- the tax credit for a student enrolled in a qualifying education program at a designated educational institution (i.e., enabled through the payment of child care or attendant care expenses);
- education and textbook tax credits;
- credit in respect of unused tax credits for tuition, education or textbooks that are transferred to the student's parent or grandparent;
- credit in respect of unused tax credits for tuition, education, age, pension and mental or physical impairment of an individual that are transferred from the individual to the individual's spouse or common-law partner;
- credit for medical expenses;
- credit for charitable donations;
- credit for interest on student loans; and
- credit in respect of the tax on dividends (see page 70, in chapter on Investment Income and Expenses).

# APPENDIX II

## Components of the Canada Child Tax Benefit (CCTB)

| | Maximum Benefit<br>Effective July 1, 2008 |
|---|---|
| **Base Benefit** | |
| Basic amount per child | $1,307 |
| Additional benefit for third child<br>and subsequent children | 91 |
| | |
| NCB Supplement: | |
| First child | 2,025 |
| Second child | 1,792 |
| Third child and subsequent children | 1,704 |
| Total CCTB benefit — Child seven years of age and over | |
| First child | 3,332 |
| Second child | 3,099 |
| Third child and subsequent children | 3,102 |
| **Changes to the Income Thresholds of the CCTB** | |
| **Base Benefit** | |
| Start phase-out | 37,885 |
| National Child Benefit (NCB) Supplement | |
| Start phase-out | 21,287 |
| End phase-out | 37,885 |

# APPENDIX III

## Marginal Tax Rates — Federal and Provincial/Territorial — 2008**

**Marginal Tax Rates — Federal — 2008**

| Taxable Income | Tax | On Next |
|---|---|---|
| $0 | $0 +15% | $37,885 |
| 37,885 | 5,683 +22% | 37,884 |
| 75,769 | 14,017 +26% | 47,415 |
| 123,184 | 26,345 + 29% | remainder |

**Marginal Tax Rates — Alberta — 2008**

| Taxable Income | Tax | On Next |
|---|---|---|
| $0 | 10% flat tax | remainder |

**Marginal Tax Rates — British Columbia — 2008**

| Taxable Income | Tax | On Next |
|---|---|---|
| $0 | $0 + 5.06% | $35,016 |
| 35,016 | 1,772 + 7.70% | 35,017 |
| 70,033 | 4,468 + 10.50% | 10,373 |
| 80,406 | 5,557 + 12.29% | 17,230 |
| 97,636 | 7,675 + 14.70% | remainder |

**Marginal Tax Rates — Manitoba — 2008**

| Taxable Income | Tax | On Next |
|---|---|---|
| $0 | $ 0 + 10.90% | $30,544 |
| 30,544 | 3,329 + 12.75% | 35,456 |
| 66,000 | 7,850 + 17.40% | remainder |

**Marginal Tax Rates — New Brunswick — 2008**

| Taxable Income | Tax | On Next |
|---|---|---|
| $0 | $0 + 10.12% | $34,836 |
| 34,836 | 3,525 + 15.48% | 34,837 |
| 69,673 | 8,918 + 16.80% | 43,600 |
| 113,273 | 16,243 + 17.95% | remainder |

## Marginal Tax Rates — Newfoundland & Labrador — 2008

| Taxable Income | Tax | On Next |
|---|---|---|
| $0 | $0 + 8.20% | $30,215 |
| 30,215 | 2,478 + 13.30% | 30,214 |
| 60,429 | 6,496 + 16.00% | remainder |

## Marginal Tax Rates — Northwest Territories — 2008

| Taxable Income | Tax | On Next |
|---|---|---|
| $0 | $0 + 5.90% | $35,986 |
| 35,986 | 2,123 + 8.60% | 35,987 |
| 71,973 | 5,218 + 12.20% | 45,038 |
| 117,011 | 10,713 + 14.05% | remainder |

## Marginal Tax Rates — Nova Scotia — 2008

| Taxable Income | Tax* | On Next |
|---|---|---|
| $$0 | $0 + 8.79% | $29,590 |
| 29,590 | 2,601 + 14.95% | 29,590 |
| 59,180 | 7,025 + 16.67% | 33,820 |
| 93,000 | 12,662 + 17.50% | remainder |

* Plus Nova Scotia surtax of 10 per cent on provincial tax above $10,000.

## Marginal Tax Rates — Nunavut — 2008

| Taxable Income | Tax | On Next |
|---|---|---|
| $0 | $0 + 4.00% | $37,885 |
| 37,885 | 1,515 + 7.00% | 37,884 |
| 75,769 | 4,167 + 9.00% | 47,415 |
| 123,184 | 8,435 + 11.50% | remainder |

## Marginal Tax Rates — Ontario — 2008

| Taxable Income | Tax* | On Next |
|---|---|---|
| $0 | $0 + 6.05% | $36,020 |
| 36,020 | 2,179 + 9.15% | 36,021 |
| 72,041 | 5,475 + 11.16% | remainder |

* Plus Ontario surtax of 20 per cent on provincial tax between $4,162 and $5,249, and an additional 36 per cent, for a total of 56 per cent, on provincial tax above $5,249.

## Marginal Tax Rates — Prince Edward Island — 2008

| Taxable Income | Tax* | On Next |
|---|---|---|
| $0 | $0 + 9.80% | $31,984 |
| 31,984 | 3,134 + 13.80% | 31,985 |
| 63,969 | 7,548 + 16.70% | remainder |

* Plus Prince Edward Island surtax of 10 per cent on provincial tax above $12,500.

## Marginal Tax Rates — Quebec — 2008

| Taxable Income | Tax | On Next |
|---:|:---:|---:|
| $0 | $0 + 16.00% | $37,500 |
| 37,500 | 6,000 + 20.00% | 37,500 |
| 75,000 | 13,500 + 24.00% | remainder |

## Marginal Tax Rates — Saskatchewan — 2008

| Taxable Income | Tax | On Next |
|---:|:---:|---:|
| $0 | $0 + 11.00% | $ 39,135 |
| 39,135 | 4,305 + 13.00% | 72,679 |
| 111,814 | 13,753 + 15.00% | remainder |

## Marginal Tax Rates — Yukon — 2008

| Taxable Income | Tax* | On Next |
|---:|:---:|---:|
| $0 | $0 + 7.04% | $37,885 |
| 37,885 | 2,667 + 9.68% | 37,884 |
| 75,769 | 6,334 + 11.44% | 47,415 |
| 123,184 | 11,759 + 12.76% | remainder |

* Plus Yukon surtax of 5 per cent on territorial tax above $6,000.

** Please note that the calculated tax payable amounts are considered to be net of any personal deductions, including non-refundable tax credits, etc. They do not take into account surtax payable, in the provinces and territories to which that applies. Surtax rates and amounts are, however, separately denoted for each relevant jurisdiction.

# APPENDIX IV

## Top Combined Federal/Provincial–Territorial Tax Rates — 2008

### Combined Top Marginal Rate (1)

| Province/ Territory | Provincial/ Territorial Rate | Ordinary Income | Capital Gains | Eligible Dividend *# | Non-Eligible Dividend *## |
|---|---|---|---|---|---|
| Alberta | 10.00% | 39.00% | 19.50% | 16.00% | 26.46% |
| British Columbia | 14.70 | 43.70 | 21.85 | 18.47 | 31.58 |
| Manitoba | 17.40 | 46.40 | 23.20 | 23.83 | 37.40 |
| New Brunswick | 17.95 | 46.95 | 23.48 | 23.18 | 35.40 |
| Newfoundland & Labrador | 16.00 | 45.00 | 22.50 | 28.11 | 33.33 |
| Northwest Territories | 14.05 | 43.05 | 21.53 | 18.25 | 29.65 |
| Nova Scotia | 17.50 | 48.25 | 24.13 | 28.35 | 33.06 |
| Nunavut | 11.50 | 40.50 | 20.25 | 22.24 | 28.96 |
| Ontario | 11.16 | 46.41 | 23.20 | 23.96 | 31.34 |
| PEI | 16.70 | 47.37 | 23.69 | 24.44 | 36.63 |
| Quebec | 24.00 | 48.22 | 24.11 | 29.69 | 36.35 |
| Saskatchewan | 15.00 | 44.00 | 22.00 | 20.35 | 30.83 |
| Yukon | 12.76 | 42.40 | 21.20 | 17.23 | 30.49 |

* Calculated on actual dividends, not grossed-up amount for tax purposes. These rates take into account the two-tier dividend tax structure introduced in 2006. Check with your Certified General Accountant to confirm which dividend rates are applicable to you.

\# Eligible dividends include those received from a public Canadian corporation and certain private, resident corporations that must pay Canadian tax at the general corporate rate.

\#\# Ineligible dividends include those received from Canadian-controlled private corporations (CCPC) that are not subject to the general corporate tax rate.

Provincial and territorial rates listed in this grouping are calculated independently of federal tax rates. In each case, lower rates apply to the lower income brackets. Note that Quebec residents receive an abatement of 16.5 per cent of the basic federal tax.

(1) Combined rates for Ordinary Income, Capital Gains and Dividend, listed above, reflect the following provincial or territorial surtaxes:

| | |
|---|---|
| Alberta | – no provincial surtaxes. |
| British Columbia | – no provincial surtaxes. |
| Manitoba | – no provincial surtaxes. |
| New Brunswick | – no provincial surtaxes. |
| Newfoundland & Labrador | – no provincial surtaxes. |
| Nova Scotia | – 10 per cent on provincial tax in excess of $10,000. |
| Ontario | – 20 per cent on provincial tax between $4,162 and $5,249, inclusive, and an additional 36 per cent, for a total of 56 per cent on provincial tax in excess of $5,249. |
| PEI | – 10 per cent on provincial tax in excess of $12,500. |
| Quebec | – no provincial surtaxes. |
| Saskatchewan | – no provincial surtaxes. |
| Northwest Territories | – no territorial surtaxes. |
| Nunavut | – no territorial surtaxes. |
| Yukon | – 5 per cent on territorial tax in excess of $6,000. |

Note: All Canadian provinces and territories, except Quebec, have adopted a "tax on income" (TONI) system of calculating provincial or territorial personal income tax. Quebec continues to administer their own provincial taxes, as they have since 1954.

# APPENDIX V

## Combined Federal and Provincial/Territorial Marginal Tax Rates for Canadian Residents — 2008 (1)

### Alberta:

| Taxable Income | Ordinary Income | Capital Gains | Eligible Dividend* | Non-Eligible Dividend* |
|---|---|---|---|---|
| At $37,885 | 32.00 | 16.00 | 5.85 | 17.71 |
| At $75,769 | 36.00 | 18.00 | 11.65 | 22.71 |
| At $123,184 | 39.00 | 19.50 | 16.00 | 26.46 |

### British Columbia:

| Taxable Income | Ordinary Income | Capital Gains | Eligible Dividend* ^ | Non-Eligible Dividend* |
|---|---|---|---|---|
| At $35,016 | 22.70 | 11.35 | (11.59) | 5.33 |
| At $37,885 | 29.70 | 14.85 | (1.83) | 14.08 |
| At $70,033 | 32.50 | 16.25 | 2.23 | 17.58 |
| At $75,769 | 36.50 | 18.25 | 8.03 | 22.58 |
| At $80,406 | 38.29 | 19.15 | 10.62 | 24.82 |
| At $97,636 | 40.70 | 20.35 | 14.12 | 27.83 |
| At $123,184 | 43.70 | 21.85 | 18.47 | 31.58 |

^ eligible dividend range of -11.59% to 0% at taxable income of $35,016
eligible dividend range of -1.83% to +4.40% at taxable income of $37,885
eligible dividend range of 2.23% to 4.40% at taxable income of $70,033
eligible dividend range of 8.03% to 10.20% at taxable income of $75,769

## Manitoba:

| Taxable Income | | Ordinary Income | Capital Gains | Eligible Dividend* ^ | Non-Eligible Dividend* |
|---|---|---|---|---|---|
| At | $30,544 | 27.75 | 13.88 | (3.21) | 14.08 |
| At | $37,885 | 34.75 | 17.38 | 6.94 | 22.83 |
| At | $66,000 | 39.40 | 19.70 | 13.68 | 28.65 |
| At | $75,769 | 43.40 | 21.70 | 19.48 | 33.65 |
| At | $123,184 | 46.40 | 23.20 | 23.83 | 37.40 |

^ eligible dividend range of -3.21% to +2.54% at taxable income of $30,544

## New Brunswick:

| Taxable Income | | Ordinary Income | Capital Gains | Eligible Dividend* ^ | Non-Eligible Dividend* |
|---|---|---|---|---|---|
| At | $34,836 | 30.48 | 15.24 | (0.70) | 14.81 |
| At | $37,885 | 37.48 | 18.74 | 9.45 | 23.56 |
| At | $69,673 | 38.80 | 19.40 | 11.36 | 25.21 |
| At | $75,769 | 42.80 | 21.40 | 17.16 | 30.21 |
| At | $113,273 | 43.95 | 21.98 | 18.83 | 31.65 |
| At | $123,184 | 46.95 | 23.48 | 23.18 | 35.40 |

^ eligible dividend range of -0.70% to 5.05% at taxable income of $34,836

## Newfoundland & Labrador:

| Taxable Income | | Ordinary Income | Capital Gains | Eligible Dividend* ^ | Non-Eligible Dividend* |
|---|---|---|---|---|---|
| At | $30,215 | 28.30 | 14.15 | 3.89 | 12.46 |
| At | $37,885 | 35.30 | 17.65 | 14.04 | 21.21 |
| At | $60,429 | 38.00 | 19.00 | 17.96 | 24.58 |
| At | $75,769 | 42.00 | 21.00 | 23.76 | 29.58 |
| At | $123,184 | 45.00 | 22.50 | 28.11 | 33.33 |

^ eligible dividend range of 3.89% to 9.64% at taxable income of $30,215

## Northwest Territories:

| Taxable Income | Ordinary Income | Capital Gains | Eligible Dividend* ^ | Non-Eligible Dividend* |
|---|---|---|---|---|
| At   $35,986 | 23.60 | 11.80 | (9.96) | 5.33 |
| At   $37,885 | 30.60 | 15.30 | 0.20 | 14.08 |
| At   $71,973 | 34.20 | 17.10 | 5.42 | 18.58 |
| At   $75,769 | 38.20 | 19.10 | 11.22 | 23.58 |
| At  $117,011 | 40.05 | 20.03 | 13.90 | 25.90 |
| At  $123,184 | 43.05 | 21.53 | 18.25 | 29.65 |

^ eligible dividend range of -9.96% to 0% at taxable income of $35,986
  eligible dividend range of 0.20% to 4.40% at taxable income of $37,885

## Nova Scotia:

| Taxable Income | Ordinary Income | Capital Gains | Eligible Dividend* ^ | Non-Eligible Dividend* |
|---|---|---|---|---|
| At   $29,590 | 29.95 | 14.98 | 3.10 | 11.15 |
| At   $37,885 | 36.95 | 18.48 | 13.25 | 19.90 |
| At   $59,180 | 38.67 | 19.34 | 15.74 | 22.05 |
| At   $75,769 | 42.67 | 21.34 | 21.54 | 27.05 |
| At   $81,105** | 44.34 | 22.17 | 22.67 | 28.17 |
| At   $93,000 | 45.25 | 22.63 | 24.00 | 29.31 |
| At  $123,184 | 48.25 | 24.13 | 28.35 | 33.06 |

^ eligible dividend range of 3.10% to 8.85% at taxable income of $29,590
** provincial surtaxes apply

## Nunavut:

| Taxable Income | Ordinary Income | Capital Gains | Eligible Dividend* | Non-Eligible Dividend* |
|---|---|---|---|---|
| At   $37,885 | 29.00 | 14.50 | 5.56 | 14.58 |
| At   $75,769 | 35.00 | 17.50 | 14.26 | 22.08 |
| At  $123,184 | 40.50 | 20.25 | 22.24 | 28.96 |

## Ontario:

| Taxable Income | | Ordinary Income | Capital Gains | Eligible Dividend* ^ | Non-Eligible Dividend* |
|---|---|---|---|---|---|
| At | $36,020 | 24.15 | 12.08 | (2.63) | 7.11 |
| At | $37,885 | 31.15 | 15.58 | 7.52 | 15.86 |
| At | $63,430** | 32.98 | 16.49 | 8.14 | 16.86 |
| At | $72,041 | 35.39 | 17.70 | 11.64 | 19.88 |
| At | $74,721** | 39.41 | 19.70 | 13.81 | 22.59 |
| At | $75,769 | 43.41 | 21.70 | 19.61 | 27.59 |
| At | $123,184 | 46.41 | 23.20 | 23.96 | 31.34 |

^ eligible dividend range of -2.63% to +3.12% at taxable income of $36,020
**provincial surtaxes apply

## Prince Edward Island:

| Taxable Income | | Ordinary Income | Capital Gains | Eligible Dividend* ^ | Non-Eligible Dividend* |
|---|---|---|---|---|---|
| At | $31,984 | 28.80 | 14.40 | (0.97) | 13.96 |
| At | $37,885 | 35.80 | 17.90 | 9.19 | 22.71 |
| At | $63,969 | 38.70 | 19.35 | 13.39 | 26.33 |
| At | $75,769 | 42.70 | 21.35 | 19.19 | 31.33 |
| At | $98,143** | 44.37 | 22.19 | 20.09 | 32.88 |
| At | $123,184 | 47.37 | 23.69 | 24.44 | 36.63 |

^ eligible dividend range of -0.97% to +4.79% at taxable income of $31,984
**provincial surtaxes apply

## Quebec:

| Taxable Income | | Ordinary Income** | Capital Gains** | Eligible Dividend** ^ | Non-Eligible Dividend** |
|---|---|---|---|---|---|
| At | $37,500 | 32.53 | 16.27 | 6.94 | 16.74 |
| At | $37,885 | 38.37 | 19.19 | 15.42 | 24.05 |
| At | $75,000 | 42.37 | 21.19 | 21.22 | 29.05 |
| At | $75,769 | 45.71 | 22.86 | 26.06 | 33.22 |
| At | $123,184 | 48.22 | 24.11 | 29.69 | 36.35 |

** Quebec residents receive an abatement of 16.5 per cent of the basic federal tax, which is factored in to the above calculations.

^ eligible dividend range of 6.94% to 11.75% at taxable income of $37,500

## Saskatchewan:

| Taxable Income | Ordinary Income | Capital Gains | Eligible Dividend* | Non-Eligible Dividend* |
|---|---|---|---|---|
| At $37,885 | 33.00 | 16.50 | 4.40 | 17.08 |
| At $39,135 | 35.00 | 17.50 | 7.30 | 19.58 |
| At $75,769 | 39.00 | 19.50 | 13.10 | 24.58 |
| At $111,814 | 41.00 | 20.50 | 16.00 | 27.08 |
| At $123,184 | 44.00 | 22.00 | 20.35 | 30.83 |

## Yukon:

| Taxable Income | Ordinary Income | Capital Gains | Eligible Dividend*^ | Non-Eligible Dividend* |
|---|---|---|---|---|
| At $37,885 | 31.68 | 15.84 | 2.49 | 17.37 |
| At $75,769 | 37.44 | 18.72 | 10.84 | 24.57 |
| At $78,755** | 38.01 | 19.01 | 10.87 | 25.01 |
| At $123,184 | 42.40 | 21.20 | 17.23 | 30.49 |

^ eligible dividend range of 2.49% to 4.40% at taxable income of $37,885
** provincial surtaxes apply

*Calculated on actual dividends, not grossed-up amount for tax purposes. These rates take into account the new two-tier dividend tax structure. Check with your Certified General Accountant to confirm which dividend rates are applicable to you.

Eligible dividends include those received from a public Canadian corporation and certain private, resident corporations that must pay Canadian tax at the general corporate rate. Note that negative rates of return for certain lower taxable income amounts, which may represent tax credits or refunds, are approximate figures only because federal tax and provincial/ territorial tax are calculated separately and cannot typically be offset against one another.

Ineligible dividends include those received from Canadian-controlled private corporations (CCPC) that are not subject to the general corporate tax rate.

(1) Federal and provincial/territorial tax rates are listed before personal credits are applied, except for rates that take into account applicable provincial/territorial surtax, as denoted by asterisk (*), which are net of the basic personal credit only. Quebec tax rates are netted off by a tax abatement of the basic federal tax of 16.5 per cent, as denoted by double asterisk (**). See Appendix 1 on page 179 for tax credit information. It is assumed each bracket is composed of ordinary income.

The rate indicated is the marginal rate for additional income of the type noted.

The above tables take into effect provincial and territorial rates. In 2008, they are as follows:

## Alberta:

Taxable Income

| | |
|---|---|
| All levels — flat tax of: | 10.00% |

Surtax: None

## British Columbia:

Taxable Income

| | |
|---|---|
| To $35,016 | 5.06% |
| From $35,016 to $70,033 | 7.70% |
| From $70,033 to $80,406 | 10.50% |
| From $80,406 to $97,636 | 12.29% |
| $97,636+ | 14.70% |

Surtax: None

## Manitoba:

Taxable Income

| | |
|---|---|
| To $34,836 | 10.90% |
| From $30,544 to $66,000 | 12.75% |
| $66,000+ | 17.40% |

Surtax: None

## New Brunswick

Taxable Income

| | |
|---|---|
| To $34,836 | 10.12% |
| From $34,836 to $69,673 | 15.48% |
| From $69,673 to $113,273 | 16.80% |
| $113,273+ | 17.95% |

Surtax: None

## Newfoundland & Labrador:

Taxable Income

| | |
|---|---|
| To $30,215 | 8.20% |
| From $30,215 to $60,429 | 13.30% |
| $60,429+ | 16.00% |

Surtax: None

## Northwest Territories:

Taxable Income

| | |
|---|---|
| To $35,986 | 5.90% |
| From $35,986 to $71,973 | 8.60% |
| From $71,973 to $117,011 | 12.20% |
| $117,011 + | 14.05% |

Surtax: None

## Nova Scotia:

Taxable Income

| | |
|---|---|
| To $29,590 | 8.79% |
| From $29,590 to $59,180 | 14.95% |
| From $59,180 to $93,000 | 16.67% |
| $93,000+ | 17.50% |

Surtax: 10 per cent of provincial tax above $10,000.

## Nunavut:

Taxable Income

| | |
|---|---|
| To $37,885 | 4.00% |
| From $37,885 to $75,769 | 7.00% |
| From $75,769 to $123,184 | 9.00% |
| $123,184+ | 11.50% |

Surtax: None

## Ontario:

Taxable Income

| | |
|---|---|
| To $36,020 | 6.05% |
| From $36,020 to $72,041 | 9.15% |
| $72,041+ | 11.16% |

Surtax: 20 per cent of provincial tax between $4,162 and $5,249, plus an additional 36 per cent, for a total of 56 per cent, for provincial tax above $5,249.

## Prince Edward Island:

Taxable Income

| | |
|---|---|
| To $31,984 | 9.80% |
| From $31,984 to $63,969 | 13.80% |
| $63,969+ | 16.70% |

Surtax: 10 per cent of provincial tax above $12,500.

## Quebec:

Taxable Income

| | |
|---|---|
| To $37,500 | 16.00% |
| From $37,500 to $75,000 | 20.00% |
| $75,000+ | 24.00% |

Surtax: None

## Saskatchewan:

Taxable Income

| | |
|---|---|
| To $39,135 | 11.00% |
| From $39,135 to $111,814 | 13.00% |
| $111,814+ | 15.00% |

Surtax: None

## Yukon:

Taxable Income

| | |
|---|---|
| To $37,885 | 7.04% |
| From $37,885 to $75,769 | 9.68% |
| From $75,769 to $123,184 | 11.44% |
| $123,184+ | 12.76% |

Surtax: 5 per cent of territorial tax above $6,000.

The tables also take into account various provincial surtaxes, as noted above.

Taxable income brackets are indexed annually by a formula based on the federal and provincial CPI increases. The above rates are therefore subject to change as a result of both that and measures brought forth in budgets introduced after the publication date.

# APPENDIX VI

## Canadian Tax Planning and Filing Deadlines — 2009*

### First Quarter

January 15      Deadline for employees who acquired qualified publicly listed shares under employee stock option plans in 2008 to file a letter indicating their intention to defer related benefits.

January 30      Pay intra-family loan interest related to previous taxation year, to avoid income attribution.

February 14      Reimburse employer for company car operating costs, to reduce operating benefit for the previous calendar year (optional). Since February 14, 2009, falls on a Saturday, it would be prudent to complete this task no later than Friday, February 13.

February 28      Last day to report personal use for previous calendar year if personal distance travelled was not greater than 20,000 kilometres and at least 50 per cent of the distance was for business purposes, in order to reduce standby charge for company car (optional). Since February 28, 2009, falls on a Saturday, it would be prudent to complete this task no later than Friday, February 27. For practical purposes, however, taxpayers who choose to make this report should really do so by mid-February.

     Last day to issue T4s, T4As and T5s to persons and the CRA. As February 28, 2009, falls on a Saturday, this deadline will automatically be extended until Monday, March 2.

March 1      Last day to make personal and spousal RRSP contributions applicable to previous taxation year. As March 1, 2009, falls on a Sunday, this deadline will automatically be extended until Monday, March 2.

| March 15 | First-quarter instalment due from taxpayers who are required to remit quarterly. As March 15, 2009, falls on a Sunday, this deadline will automatically be extended until Monday, March 16. |
| March 31 | File Trust Income Tax Return for trusts with a December 31 year end. |

## Second Quarter

| April 30 | File Personal Income Tax return for previous taxation year and remit balance due, if any, to the CRA. |
| | File GST rebate application for employee-related expenses deducted in previous taxation year. |
| June 15 | Second-quarter instalment due from taxpayers who are required to remit quarterly. |
| | Due date for personal tax returns of individuals with self-employed business income, or spouses/common-law partners of taxpayers with self-employed business income. (Payment of tax balance still due April 30.) |

## Third Quarter

| September 15 | Third-quarter instalment due from taxpayers who are required to remit quarterly. |

## Fourth Quarter

| December 15 | Fourth-quarter instalment due from taxpayers who are required to remit quarterly. |
| December 31 | Annual tax instalment due from individuals whose chief source of income is farming or fishing, and who choose not to remit quarterly. |
| | Deadline for taxpayers age 71 (born in 1938) to ensure 2009 contributions to their own RRSP are made. It is also the deadline for such individuals to convert their RRSPs to either RRIFs or life annuities. (People in that situation should, however, consult a Certified General Accountant who practices personal financial planning well in advance of that date to discuss the various options available to them.) |

Deadline for taxpayers who qualify to have the operating cost benefit with respect to an automobile used for employment, calculated as half the amount of the annual standby charge, to notify their employer in writing of such intentions.

Ensure tax-deductible fees (e.g., accounting, investment counsel, interest carrying charges and safety deposit box), expenses (e.g., employee-related moving expenses) and credits (e.g., for charitable donations and medical expenses) for the current taxation year have been paid.

* Federal deadlines only. Consult your provincial or territorial Finance or equivalent ministry to determine relevant provincial/territorial tax filing deadlines.

# APPENDIX VII

## Prescribed CRA Interest Rates
## on Overdue and Unpaid Income Taxes

| | Federal | | |
| --- | --- | --- | --- |
| | **Receiver General Payments** | | **All Other** |
| | **To** | **From** | **Purposes** |
| 2007 – 1st quarter | 9% | 7% | 5% |
| 2nd quarter | 9 | 7 | 5 |
| 3rd quarter | 9 | 7 | 5 |
| 4th quarter | 9 | 7 | 5 |
| 2008 – 1st quarter | 8% | 6% | 4% |
| 2nd quarter | 8 | 6 | 4 |
| 3rd quarter | 7 | 5 | 3 |
| 4th quarter | 7 | 5 | 3 |

# APPENDIX VIII

## Glossary of Abbreviations and Acronyms

| | |
|---|---|
| ABE | Adult basic education |
| ABIL | Allowable business investment loss |
| ACB | Adjusted cost base |
| AIDA | Agricultural income disaster assistance |
| AMPA | *Agricultural Marketing Programs Act* |
| AMT | Alternative minimum tax |
| APF | Agricultural policy framework |
| AVC | Additional voluntary contribution |
| CAIS | Canadian Agricultural Income Stabilization program |
| CCA | Capital cost allowance |
| CCPC | Canadian-controlled private corporation |
| CRA | Canada Revenue Agency |
| CCTB | Canada child tax benefit |
| CDB | Child disability benefit |
| CDNX | Canadian venture exchange |
| CDSB | Canada disability savings bond |
| CDSG | Canada disability savings grant |
| CESG | Canada education savings grant |
| CFBAS | Canadian Farm Business Advisory Services |
| CNIL | Cumulative net investment loss |
| CPI | Consumer price index |
| CPP | Canada Pension Plan |
| CRCE | Canadian renewable and conservation expenses |
| DOF | Department of Finance |
| DPSP | Deferred profit-sharing plan |
| DRIP | Dividend reinvestment plan |
| DSLP | Deferred salary leave plan |
| DTC | Disability tax credit |
| EAP | Education assistance payments |

| | |
|---|---|
| EHT | Employer health tax |
| EI | Employment insurance |
| EO-LSVCC | Employee ownership labour-sponsored venture capital corporation |
| FCA | Federal Court of Appeal |
| FMV | Fair market value |
| GAAR | General anti-avoidance rule |
| GIC | Guaranteed investment certificate |
| GIS | Guaranteed income supplement |
| GST | Goods and services tax |
| GSTC | Goods and services tax credit |
| GTE | Graduate tax exemption (Saskatchewan) |
| HBP | Home buyers' plan |
| HST | Harmonized sales tax |
| IC | Information circular |
| IPP | Individual pension plans |
| IRS | Internal Revenue Service (U.S.) |
| ITC | Investment tax credit |
| LIF | Life income fund |
| LIRA | Locked-in retirement account |
| LLP | Lifelong learning plan |
| LP | Limited partnership |
| LRIF | Locked-in retirement income fund |
| LSIF | Labour-sponsored investment fund |
| LSVCC | Labour-sponsored venture capital corporation |
| LTT | Land transfer tax |
| MIA | Mandatory inventory adjustment |
| MURB | Multiple-unit residential building |
| NCB | National child benefit |
| OAS | Old age security |
| OCB | Ontario child benefit |
| OCCS | Ontario child care supplement |
| OETC | Overseas employment tax credit |
| OIA | Optional inventory adjustment |
| PA | Pension adjustment |
| PAR | Pension adjustment reversal |

| | |
|---|---|
| PHSP | Private health services plan |
| PRIF | Prescribed retirement income fund |
| PSPA | Past service pension adjustment |
| PST | Provincial sales tax |
| QFP | Qualified farm property |
| QPIP | Quebec Parental Insurance Plan |
| QPP | Quebec Pension Plan |
| R&D | Research and development |
| RCA | Retirement compensation arrangement |
| RDSP | Registered disability savings plan |
| REOP | Reasonable expectation of profit |
| RESP | Registered education savings plan |
| RLIF | Restricted life income fund |
| RLSP | Restricted locked-in savings plan |
| RPP | Registered pension plan |
| RRIF | Registered retirement income fund |
| RRSP | Registered retirement savings plan |
| SBC | Small business corporation |
| SIFT | Specified investment flow-through |
| SIN | Social insurance number |
| SR&ED | Scientific research and experimental development |
| TCC | Tax Court of Canada |
| TFSA | Tax-free savings account |
| TONI | Tax on income |
| UCC | Undepreciated capital cost |
| UCCB | Universal child care benefit |
| UL | Universal life |
| VDP | Voluntary Disclosures Program |
| WITB | Working income tax benefit |
| WSIB | Workplace Safety and Insurance Board |

# Index

# FOR MORE INFORMATION

If you have any questions that this book doesn't answer, or would like more information on how a CGA can help you or your business, contact CGA-Canada or your local provincial/territorial CGA Association.

**CGA-Canada**
100 - 4200 North Fraser Way
Burnaby, BC  V5J 5K7
T    604 669-3555
F    604 689-5845
www.cga.org/canada

**CGA-Canada Ottawa Office**
1201 – 350 Sparks Street
Ottawa, ON  K1R 7S8
T    613 789-7771
F    613 789-7772
E    ottawa@cga-canada.org

**CGA-Hong Kong**
Room 3506, Tower 1
Unit A, 10/F, 211 Johnston Road
Wanchai, Hong Kong
T    852 2858-1712
F    852 2559-4536
E    info@cgahk.org.hk
www.cgahk.org.hk

**Beijing Representation Office**
c/o Techscien Professional
Education Institute
Room 304, Tower B, Jia Li Building
180 Beiyuanlu, Chaoyang District
Beijing 100101, P.R. China
T    8610 6491-6570
     8610 6491-6571
F    8610 6492-1279
E    edubj@cga-china.org
www.cga-online.org/cn

**Shanghai Representation Office**
c/o Techscien Professional
Education Institute
7G, Apong Mansion,
585 Ling Ling Road
Shanghai 200030, P.R. China
T   86 21 6468-6541
F   86 21 6439-3298
E   edush@cga-china.org
www.cga-online.org/cn

**Zhuhai Representation Office**
c/o Techscien Professional
Education Institute
Building 30, Australia Villa,
No. 2 Longxing Street
Jiuzhou Avenue
Zhuhai 519015, P.R. China
T   86 756 813-7903
F   86 756 813-7902
E   eduzh@cga-china.org
www.cga-online.org/cn

**Guangzhou Representation Office**
c/o Techscien Professional
Education Institute
Room 1203, No. 11 Tiahe Road
Dongshan District
Guangzhou 510075, P.R. China
T   86 20 3760-3630
F   86 20 3760-4030
E   edugz@cga-china.org
www.cga-online.org/cn

**CGA-Bahamas**
P.O. Box N-7777
29 Retirement Road
3 Shirley Street
Nassau, Bahamas
T   242 393-0224
F   242 393-7570
E   louibt@bahamas.net.bs
www.cga-online.org/bs

**CGA Caribbean Region**
CGA Student Services Inc.
Suite 23, In-One-Accord Plaza
Warrens, St. Michael
Barbados
T   246 424-8617
      246 424-8596
F   246 424-8496
E   publiccga@cga-barbados.org
www.cga-online.org/bb

**St. Lucia Representation Office**
c/o IBT Inc.
P.O. Box 1777, L'Anse Road, Castries, St. Lucia
T   758 451-6675
F   758 451-6674
E   ibt@candw.lc
www.cga-online.org/bb

**Trinidad and Tobago Representation Office**
c/o RBTT ROYTEC
136 – 138 Henry Street, Port of Spain, Trinidad
T   868 627-8553
F   868 623-7338
E   registrar@roytec.com
www.cga-online.org/bb

**CGA-Bermuda**
Vallis Building, Ground Floor
46 Par-la-Ville Road, Hamilton HM 11, Bermuda
T   441 292-9078
F   441 295-9462
E   cgabermuda@northrock.bm
www.cga-online.org/bm

**CGA-Yukon Territory**
P.O. Box 5358
Whitehorse, Yukon  Y1A 4Z2
T     867 668-4461
F     867 667-5790

**CGA-Northwest Territories/Nunavut**
P.O. Box 128
5016 50th Avenue, 3rd Floor
Yellowknife, NWT  X1A 2N1
T    867 873-5620
F    867 873-4469
www.cga-nwt-nu.org

**CGA-British Columbia**
1867 West Broadway, 3rd Floor
Vancouver, BC  V6J 5L4
T    604 732-1211
F    604 732-9439
www.cga-online.org/bc

**CGA-Alberta**
100 - 325 Manning Road NE
Calgary, AB  T2E 2PS
T    403 299-1300
F    403 299-1339
www.cga-online.org/ab

**CGA Saskatchewan**
4 – 2345 Avenue C North
Saskatoon, SK  S7L 5Z5
T    306 955-4622
F    306 373-9219
www.cga-online.org/sk

**CGA-Manitoba**
4 Donald Street South
Winnipeg, MB  R3L 2T7
T    204 477-1256
F    204 453-7176
www.cga-online.org/mb

**CGA Ontario**
240 Eglinton Avenue East
Toronto, ON  M4P 1K8
T    416 322-6520
F    416 322-5594
www.cga-ontario.org

**Ordre des CGA du Québec**
445, boul. St-Laurent, Bureau 450
Montréal, QC  H2Y 2Y7
T    514 861-1823
F    514 861-7661
www.cga-quebec.org

**CGA-New Brunswick**
10 – 236 St. George Street
Moncton, NB  E1C 1W1
T    506 857-0939
F    506 855-0887
www.cga-online.org/nb

**CGA Nova Scotia**
P.O. Box 73 CRO
Halifax, NS  B3J 2L4
T    902 425-4923
F    902 425-4983
www.cga-ns.org

**CGA-Prince Edward Island**
P.O. Box 20151
Charlottetown, PEI  C1A 9E3
T    902 368-7237
F    902 368-3627
www.cga-online.org/pe

**CGA-Newfoundland and Labrador**
201 – 294 Freshwater Road
St. John's, NL  A1B 1C1
T    709 579-1863
F    709 579-0838
www.cga-online.org/nl

**CGA Student Services**
Maritime Region Inc.
P.O. Box 5100
403 – 236 St. George Street
Moncton, NB  E1C 8R2
T    506 857-2204
F    506 852-4450
www.cga-maritime.org

# NOTES